LET EV
PRAISE

MW01204712

MURPHY CHURCH

Need to talk to someone? Need someone to
pray for you? Murphy Church is here for you.

Please contact us:
972.424.6026 | office@murphychurch.com

LET EVERYTHING THAT HATH BREATH PRAISE THE LORD

LET EVERYTHING THAT HATH BREATH PRAISE THE LORD

www.diggingawell.blogspot.com

CONTENTS

CONTENTS CONTINUED

CONTENTS CONTINUED

CONTENTS CONTINUED

ACKNOWLEDGEMENTS

Fay Palmer took the time out of her schedule to proof and correct each devotion. Fay has been there for me every time there was a need. She gives unconditionally each time, whether it is sewing wedding dresses or proofing books.

Bobbie Dale Cotton has a servant heart that is revealed in each area of the ministry at Northside Baptist Church. She has always been willing to help wherever the need arises.

Balinda Zimmerman has spent many hours helping me with the layouts, graphics and proofing of the books. She has encouraged me to keep on writing when I felt like giving up.

Lisa, my daughter, this year for Mother's Day gave of herself. She has spent months helping me with the final proofing.

Steve, my husband, who listened to me endlessly working the details of my blog and books, from my heart and mind onto paper. He has spend many hours proofing each piece of work.

Prayer warriors from six different states have lifted me up in prayer and helped me to complete that which the Lord began.

LET EVERYTHING THAT HATH BREATH PRAISE THE LORD

FORWARD

I have had the honor and privilege of being one of the original members of "Digging the Well Ministries."

God sent Sherry into my life at a time when I was seeking and searching as to how God could use me in *his* work.

Sherry is the type of person who looks at you, your talents and your gifts with her whole heart, then seeks God's leadership on how to better encourage you to get busy serving the Lord.

One good way to follow our gracious Lord and Savior is a daily devotional study. A daily walk with the Lord is a blessing, and devotionals play a big part in guiding us in this daily walk.

Devotionals can speak to us in many ways and through a wide range of subject matter. As you read each devotional, allow the Lord to open not only your mind but also your heart as you seek to better understand what our Lord and Savior has in store for you.

I pray each of these devotionals will encourage us to live and learn how we can be better prepared to help others in their daily walk with the Lord.

Fay Palmer

You will never discover
how far the Lord
will take you in the
journey of life,
until you take
the first step.

LIGHTS ON! EVERYONE

Today I went outside and took all my Christmas decorations down. I started with the snowman painting on my front door. I tucked it away into a box along with the fat fluffy snowman that sat on my front porch.

Next, I moved to the mailbox and removed all the lights tightly wrapped around it.

Lastly, I removed the netted lights from my shrubs and removed the lights off the five trees. The top of the house didn't get decorated this year so at least the project didn't take as long as usual.

As I stood and looked at my house, it was almost as if it had a frown. So bare and unappealing it looked to me. I was already missing the lights, glistening at night.

Softly, the Lord spoke to my heart and said, "Look a little deeper, this house shines to the world with the light of Jesus, not just one month out of a year but all year long."

My heart then settled as I realized that the light of Jesus Christ is what we desire to portray to the world during the holiday season.

What an awesome feeling settled over me as I realized I now have lights that can shine all over the world, all year round. Lights on everyone!

Ye have not chosen me, but I have chosen you, and ordained you, that ye should go and bring forth fruit, and that your fruit should remain: that whatsoever ye shall ask of the Father in my name, he may give it you. (John 15:16)

SOLAR LIGHTS SHOW US HOW MUCH WE NEED THE SON

I have a lot of solar lights in my front yard and around the top of my above the ground swimming pool. I am able to go out at dark and swim and see the beauty of my backyard, because of all the solar lights.

One thing I learned about solar lights - if they do not receive the sun rays, they will not shine at night. Our lives are the same as the solar lights. We need the constant light of Jesus shining on us in order to endure the hardships and times of darkness that pass through our lives.

There will be times our friends and families will go through hardships. We might pick up our light, run to them, and want to help them through their trials.

If we get there and our light is not shining, what have we accomplished?

In order to fully help those in need, we need to allow ourselves to soak up the *Son* and absorb his love and compassion. When we get ready to help other's they will be able to see the light of Jesus shining through us.

Let your light so shine before men, that they may see your good works, and glorify your Father which is in heaven. (Matthew 5:16)

REPOTTING YOUR FAITH

Have you ever noticed a plant in a small flower pot? It can grow and be beautiful but it will only grow as far as the little pot allows. There comes a time that the plant gets root bound and the growth is halted.

For many years I had plants but didn't understand the concept of repotting, not understanding that the fresh soil and larger pot enhanced new growth.

Sometimes we are like these plants. We need to repot our faith, remove it from its original container – shake the soil loose and study it to see if it needs more nutritious soil added to the mixture.

Allow the Lord to be the Master Gardener and help you find his word to be fresh, new and exciting. Today is a good day to go on a shopping spree through the scriptures and find that new soil?

Perhaps you have used many scriptures for twenty years or more. They are great scriptures, and you don't want to throw them out but what you need to do is find some fresh ones to add to the pot.

Your faith may have previously been placed in the smallest container possible. Plant your faith in something larger than you have ever done before. Go ahead, try it!

Make a list of areas where you need to have a greater faith. Place your heart in those areas and watch your faith grow.

Rooted and built up in him, and stablished in the faith, as ye have been taught, abounding therein with thanksgiving. (Colossians 2:7)

PRAISE OR POUT?

On the way to work one Friday, I was praying about something that bothered me. I told the Lord:

"You know we all have a choice. We can either Praise or Pout when we don't get our way."

I asked the Lord,

"Does it really make a difference if we praise or pout?" Obviously I wanted to have a pouting session myself.

This is what the Lord showed me: If you take the *P* and put it in front of the word *raise* you get the word *praise*. If people see us begin praising, it will begin to raise others up.

People love to be around others who lift them up. Souls can be reached and we become more likely to be able to mentor others and help them become great leaders.

If you take the *P* and put it in front of *"out,"* you get *pout*. If we pout then people want out. We lose our testimony and in turn lose the chance to witness and mentor others.

When we pout, people also want out of our lives and will definitely not want what we're sharing. If what you are sharing is Jesus, make sure people find your life appealing.

Stop and fill in the blank where you intend to place the *P*.

_RAISE

_OUT

*Rejoice in the Lord alway: and again I say, Rejoice.
(Philippians 4:4)*

4

GOD'S TELEPHONE NUMBER

As parents and grandparents we teach our children the importance of knowing their home or cell phone number. We also teach them how to dial 911 in case of an emergency. It's important for them to know how to find their house and how to tell the police their address in case they get lost. There are many things children need to learn about safety.

When I was a young child my mother taught me how to find my way home and what my address was but she didn't stop there. My mother knew the importance of my knowing how to call and find my way to the Lord Jesus Christ during a crisis. She would often ask me what the Lord's telephone number was.

It is important that we instill this into our children's lives. To this day, if I find myself in a crisis, I am reminded to call on the Lord.

I am thankful for the verse my mother repeatedly taught me so I would have access to my Father God, at all times.

> *Call unto me, and I will answer thee, and shew thee great and mighty things, which thou knowest not.*
>
> *(Jeremiah 33:3)*

THE HORSESHOE – HOW TO PREPARE OUR FEET FOR THE MINISTRY

When we lived in Ignacio, Colorado we used to go up Missionary Ridge, outside of Durango Colorado, and round up cattle. We would begin before sunrise and have all the cattle brought down the mountain by midnight.

The mountain was steep and rugged. It required that the horses be prepared for the event. The Faverinos, the ranch owners, would go to great lengths to make sure the horseshoes were solid and secure, the saddles were proper, and each horse was strong enough to endure the elements needed for the roundup.

With all the preparation needed for their horses, it surprises me to know that wild horses do not need horseshoes. It seems they would need horseshoes more than their domesticated kin.

The elements of their lives do not consist of protection, softness or relaxation. Living in the rough terrain continually is what keeps the horses from needing their feet shod. Their hooves stay hardened due to the roughness of the terrain.

Once a horse has been domesticated it takes on a new life. The horse is brushed, put into fenced areas with soft luscious grass, and given a stable with hay and shelter against the storms. Because of all the protection it is given, its hooves become softer. As the hooves soften, the horse's daily chores become painful. It begins to have pain shoot up its legs due to the softness of the hooves.

In order for the horse to be able to function properly, the craftsman has to come along and put horseshoes on its feet to

6

prevent the horse from becoming crippled. After the craftsman performs this task, the horse is ready to handle just about anything.

Before you came to know Christ, you were much like a wild horse. Your life was hardened and your daily routine kept it that way. You were unaware of the love of God and his provisions.

Once you came to know Christ, you were removed from the elements that kept you rough and hardened. Now, you have entered into God's presence where there is rest and comfort.

When you go back out into the world, it will not be as before. You are sheltered in the arms of God and safe from life's storms This doesn't mean you will not experience any storms in life but when the storms come, God will be there as a place of refuge for you. Just as the horse now has a stable, the Lord will be a place of refuge in which to keep you safe from life's storms.

When you go back into the rough terrain, you now need to prepare differently.

If there were snow on the ground, would you need to be wearing your Diva peeped toe heel pumps? No, we must prepare our day for the things we will be facing.

Living in Colorado, I had to make sure I had my heavy snow boots on when stepping outside into the elements or my feet would soon be frozen.

Upon first arriving to Colorado, I tried my pumps on the snow and ice and my bumps and bruises taught me to prepare differently the next time I ventured out.

"Having your feet shod with the preparation of the gospel of peace" as the scripture says. This is something you need to do daily, just as you would put on your regular shoes. If you

were preparing for a normal day, you would ask yourself this question, "What is the weather going to be like?"

The same is true with your spiritual life. You need to prepare for the elements you will face during the day. Don't start your day without putting on the whole armor of God.

Satan wants more than ever to draw us back into the wild. If we are not grounded in the word of God, our feet will slip easily back into his traps of deception and rough terrain.

Finally, my brethren, be strong in the Lord, and in the power of his might. Put on the whole armour of God, that ye may be able to stand against the wiles of the devil. For we wrestle not against flesh and blood, but against principalities, against powers, against the rulers of the darkness of this world, against spiritual wickedness in high places. Wherefore take unto you the whole armour of God, that ye may be able to withstand in the evil day, and having done all, to stand. Stand therefore, having your loins girt about with truth, and having on the breastplate of righteousness; And your feet shod with the preparation of the gospel of peace; above all, taking the shield of faith, wherewith ye shall be able to quench all the fiery darts of the wicked. And take the helmet of salvation, and the sword of the Spirit, which is the word of God: Praying always with all prayer and supplication in the Spirit, and watching thereunto with all perseverance and supplication for all saints; (Ephesians 6:10-18)

THE CATERPILLAR TEACHES US THE UPS AND DOWNS OF LIFE

Do the ups and downs get to you?

Have you experienced these two opposite contrasts in your lifetime?

There's not a one of us who has had as many ups and downs as the caterpillar. Take the time to watch him as he moves. Every step requires his body to go up and down many times. This little guy just keeps on pushing forward even with all the ups and downs.

He never gives up.

Rejoicing in hope; patient in tribulation; continuing instant in prayer; (Romans 12:12)

We need to be more like the caterpillar, setting our eyes on a goal. No matter what gets in front of us, no matter how many times situations gets us down, just keep on keeping on – knowing the end result is far greater than the pain we are enduring.

Parents, there is a valuable lesson here in rearing your children also. If the caterpillar never experiences the traumatic stages of life, he will never develop into a beautiful butterfly.

When you are a helicopter mom or dad, meaning one that hovers over your children, this can be harmful to your child.

You don't want them experiencing anything bad so you shelter them from daily battles. This act keeps them from developing fully.

It's the ups and downs and the hard things in life that shape and prepare the child for a greater life.

Before changing into a beautiful butterfly, the caterpillar has to experience the different stages of struggles in its life.

After this creature has gone through the trials of daily living, one day it will attach itself to a branch and spin silk around itself. The caterpillar appears to be motionless inside of this cocoon. Even though we can't see what is taking place, one of the most awesome transformations is occurring. It will emerge from its cocoon and we will be able to see its magnificent beauty.

This little creature still isn't finished with the process of its ups and downs. If the caterpillar stopped at this stage and did not complete the last step, it would never fly.

The caterpillar must still go through one enormous struggle. Once it emerges from the cocoon, sitting with its wings hanging downward, attached to the cocoon, it starts to pump fluid through its wings.

One breath, two breaths, "Ah, that should do it." No, it must keep this process up for close to two hours! When it has completed all these struggles, that's when this magnificent creature is ready to spread its wings for the adventure of a lifetime.

When we attach ourselves to the Lord Jesus Christ, he will help us go through all of those struggles we face. There will be nothing that can stop us from being like the caterpillar that has gone through metamorphosis – beautiful, fully equipped with what we need, ready to do the Lord's service.

Nay, in all these things we are more than conquerors through him that loved us. For I am persuaded, that neither death, nor life, nor angels, nor principalities, nor powers, nor things present, nor things to come, Nor height, nor depth, nor any other creature, shall be able to separate us from the love of God, which is in Christ Jesus our Lord. (Romans 8:37-39)

U R THE DIFFERENCE IN NATURE VERSUS NURTURE

Have you ever heard the argument of "Nature versus Nurture?"

"Nature" is what we naturally would do on our own. "Nurture" is the things we do because we have people in our lives leading and guiding us.

Some argue we are who we are because of our natural disposition. Others argue we do the things we do because of the things we have been taught.

U R the difference between nature and nurture. U R the one who can make a difference in others' lives. A child who is brought up in a home well nurtured will be more capable in the work place and more able to succeed in life.

Those who have been nurtured in the word of God are better able to stand against the wiles of the devil. U R the one who needs to be doing the nurturing.

What happens to children left to rear themselves? They have more of a tendency to their natural ways.

The scriptures warn us about this. Our nature is characteristically sinful. As I watch my grandchildren, as adorable and sweet as they are, I can see the sin nature trying to rear its head.

They need the nurturing of their parents, grandparents, aunts, uncles, and teachers in order to bring them up in the admonition of the Lord.

Did this verse say "fathers" because they are the only ones to do it? No, but the father, being the head of the house, needs to set the pattern and guide his family in the right direction.

There is a huge responsibility on the fathers to set the pace for his family to follow. Remember, whether male or female, U R the one that can make a difference in the world around you, as you nurture your children.

Children, obey your parents in the Lord: for this is right. Honour thy father and mother; (which is the first commandment with promise;) That it may be well with thee, and thou mayest live long on the earth. And, ye fathers, provoke not your children to wrath: but bring them up in the nurture and admonition of the Lord. (Ephesians 6:1-4)

THE GIRAFFE TEACHES US TO STRETCH

Today I was sending a friend a text about my upcoming book signings that will be held in Sweetwater, Texas and Andrews, Texas where I graduated from High School. I shared with my friend, "I never feel like I meet up to the expectation that I place on myself. I am always stretching to be better at each thing I do, whether it's writing, singing, playing the piano or cooking. I always seem to fall short of the mark I have set. Most of the time, I fall way short of that mark."

This caused me to start thinking about the giraffe.[1] The giraffe is the tallest land mammal. The male giraffe can grow up to eighteen feet in height, with the female only slightly smaller. Their neck span can be up to seven feet long. This doesn't keep the giraffe from trying to stretch even taller in order to retrieve food that is seen high up in the trees. The male will stretch as far as his long neck will allow in search of the most nutritious leaves he is able to retrieve. The female will settle for food that is slightly lower in order to keep from having to stretch. Thus making both animals satisfied with not being in each other's path.

It is my desire that I will continue to have the drive to learn to write, spell and correct my grammar more proficiently each time I write.

Most important, however, is that I share the gospel of Jesus Christ in a way that others can understand and come to know the Lord as their Savior I want to never get in the way of others

---

[1] http://www.howtallisagiraffe.com/

just as the female giraffe shows but allow others to reach the heights of their God given abilities.

I want to be like the giraffe; always stretching for the most nutritious food, never settling for anything less than the most nourishing things the Lord places before us each day.

Study to shew thyself approved unto God, a workman that needeth not to be ashamed, rightly dividing the word of truth. But shun profane and vain babblings: for they will increase unto more ungodliness. (II Timothy 2:15-16)

TIMES OF DROUGHT

Do you ever have dry seasons in your life? If not, you are an exception to the rule. I have had many times in my life that I have experienced these seasons of drought.

There are people who believe and teach that we should never experience a dry season and should only experience springtime, filled with abundance and joy continually. It would be nice to experience springtime year round but the fact remains, we are going to have times of drought. As we watch people who believe and teach we should never have times of drought, we will see and testify they too have dry periods in their lives.

There is nothing wrong with finding ourselves in a dry season but we constantly need to remember that during these times we still have the aquifer, the Lord Jesus Christ, as the constant supply for our thirst.

There are times that we must dig deeper in order to find the water source, but knowing that it is always there is a great comfort.

The West Texas land is dry and barren but if we were to drop down several hundred feet, we would find the aquifer, a constant supply of water. Even though the land is visibly dry, there is an abundance of water that could be brought to the surface.

The same is true in our lives. We may appear to be in a time of drought but if we dig deep enough into the word of God, we also will find the aquifer for our soul. Often, the seasons of drought are followed by a plenteous season. Once again, we can flourish as in the springtime.

15

LET EVERYTHING THAT HATH BREATH PRAISE THE LORD

The wilderness and the solitary place shall be glad for them; and the desert shall rejoice, and blossom as the rose. (Isaiah 35:1)

But they that wait
upon the LORD
shall renew their strength;
they shall mount up
with wings as eagles;
they shall run,
and not be weary;
and they shall walk,
and not faint.
Isaiah 40:31

HOW DO YOU GAUGE YOUR LIFE?

For the last two weeks I have been having trouble with my truck's instrument panel. It seems that either all the controls work, or none of them work.

Switching out all the fuses and putting a new battery on the truck didn't help. The bottom line is: My truck is not trustworthy. Until I can figure out what it needs, the truck will continue to be untrustworthy.

Do you ever feel your life is like this?

We may go through life feeling as though we have nothing to use as a guide. We may feel our lives have no direction.

We need the word of God as our instrument panel. Within God's word is everything necessary for all life's situations. The Holy Spirit will be our gauge. He will lead, guide and comfort us.

How often do you look to your Spiritual instrument control for guidance?

We need the word of God to show us if we are moving in the wrong direction, going too fast or too slow. When we look to the Spirit of God for our guidance, then he will faithfully lead us.

The Lord will not be like the instrument panel in my truck that only works part of the time. He is faithfully there.

Let us hold fast the profession of our faith without wavering; (for he is faithful that promised;)
(Hebrews 10:23)
For as many as are led by the Spirit of God, they are the sons of God. (Romans 8:14)

ARE YOU COMBINING THE RIGHT INGREDIENTS?

Did you know that yeast is alive? Living organisms need food. Even though this ingredient is alive, it will do nothing until the correct ingredient is added to it. You can add flour, water and yeast together, cook it, and your product will come out flat. This is called unleavened. You can add salt to the mixture and you will get the same result. The one ingredient that makes a change in the appearance of yeast is sugar.

If you take the same ingredients and add sugar, instantly a change begins to take place. The process of fermentation begins. Before your eyes, the mixture will start to grow. Within a couple hours, the mixture will double.

How many times have we had faith and no results? In our Christian lives we may be doing the same thing. We may be combining the wrong ingredients and yet expecting the Lord to give us increase. If you want to see your Christian walk rise to new heights be sure to mix the right ingredients.

You might say, "What ingredients are you talking about?"

We are saved by faith in the Lord Jesus Christ but what is the one ingredient that shows the world we are saved. It is when they see something active in our lives that they know we are serving a living Savior and not one that is dead. In order for others to see our faith, they must see our works.

Belief isn't enough. The devils believe but they don't reach out and take the gift, nor do they put the gift to action.

Belief is trust that Evel Knievel can jump the Grand Canyon. Faith is climbing onto the bike with him. You are showing action when you climb on the bike yourself.

The Lord is looking for the right ingredients in your life. Have you merely been living a life of "belief" or a life of true faith and trust? Let's start mixing the right ingredients and see what the Lord does in our lives.

Even so faith, if it hath not works, is dead, being alone. Yea, a man may say, Thou hast faith, and I have works: shew me thy faith without thy works, and I will shew thee my faith by my works. Thou believest that there is one God; thou doest well: the devils also believe, and tremble. But wilt thou know, O vain man, that faith without works is dead? (James 2:17-20)

For by grace are ye saved through faith; and that not of yourselves: it is the gift of God: Not of works, lest any man should boast. For we are his workmanship, created in Christ Jesus unto good works, which God hath before ordained we should walk in them. (Ephesians 4:8-9)

Read Hebrews Chapter 11 about people who lived by faith. You will notice each of these individuals did something during their lives that caused them to be chosen for the "Hall of Faith." You will see that they all didn't do the same thing. They all did the thing the Lord asked them to do. What is the one thing the Lord is asking you to do so others will see your faith?

ARE YOU SEARCHING FOR GOODNESS OR GOD?

When we start Kindergarten, we learn some basic things such as how to tell the difference between two objects. We learn which objects match and those that do not.

The same is true with the word of God. There are certain things in our lives we can match one to the other.

The one concept people tend to mismatch is goodness. When we try to match goodness with anything but God, it is incorrect.

The word "goodness" comes from the root word "good," which means "morally excellent."

One of the things God said after he created each day was, "It is good." In other words, he was saying it pleased him. So we see the word "good" pleases God.

When he created mankind He said, "It is very good."

When God referred to his creation it was truly at the stage of perfection. It had not been tainted by sin. When he created mankind, he didn't say, "It is good." He said, "It is very good." The scriptures also say we were created in the image of God. We were created pure, holy and righteous before the Father.

The scriptures refer to God as being good. If this is true, then we can say goodness refers to holy, pure and right.

O give thanks unto the LORD; for he is good: for his mercy endureth for ever. (Psalm 136:1)

And Jesus said unto him, Why callest thou me good? there is none good but one, that is, God. (Mark 10:18)

21

STEERING WHEELS
AND U-TURNS

What do you keep before your eyes? Where do you allow your hands to take you? The thing that is set before you is what will likely guide your life.

It has been said many times, "Let me see your checkbook and I will tell you the things you love." The scriptures say, "Out of the abundance of man's heart the mouth speaks." Whatever we feed ourselves with will be what comes forth from our mouth. The steering wheel in your hands will follow your heart.

This has been something I have pondered for several weeks now. It is something that is strong on my heart. Because the things I see us putting before our eyes are not godly things.

There is a house that sat straight across from the hospital in the town where I lived. Before the previous owners moved out, it had a huge sign with the Ten Commandments on it. This is actually what the bible says we are to do in Proverbs. It says we are to keep the word of God before our eyes. We are to put it on the doorpost of our houses; we are to bind them on our fingers and to write them on the tablets of our heart.

We have many Christian plaques on the walls inside of our home, but that is not enough. We are to keep them between our eyes; we are to bind them on our fingertips. We are to learn them and have them written on our hearts. They are to be visible everywhere we look.

We are a generation that has failed to do this and the proof is becoming obvious every day. I have walked into the bedrooms of many teenagers over the last ten to fifteen years. What I am seeing posted on their walls is not the word of God.

LET EVERYTHING THAT HATH BREATH PRAISE THE LORD

I have worked with many men in the oilfield who profess Jesus Christ but what they have posted on the panels of their trucks is not the word of God. If we were to check the computers of every Christian home in America, what would we find? Would there be times our fingers did the walking on the keyboards and because of it our computers show pictures of nudity?

Why are we allowing our steering wheels to be turned toward ungodly things? Our steering wheels have not only turned to strange women but now we are the ones giving them free advertisement on our computers and television sets.

We have men that profess to be Christians telling their boys, "This is a good thing and something real men do." When you teach this to your children it is like pulling trash out of the dumpster and telling them to eat it. You are not teaching them wisdom but destruction.

The world has lied to us and we have believed that lie. Marriages are being torn apart daily because of what men are posting in front of their eyes. It is time we grab the steering wheel, and do a u-turn with our lives and lead our family and friends to follow.

The scriptures tell in the book of Proverbs which path to follow. If this is so, why are we teaching our children that real men go this other way? Let's teach them when it's time to do a u-turn and to put the right things before their eyes.

My son, keep my words, and lay up my commandments with thee. Keep my commandments, and live; and my law as the apple of thine eye. Bind them upon thy fingers, write them upon the table of thine heart. Say unto wisdom, Thou art my sister; and call understanding thy kinswoman: That they may keep thee from the strange woman, from the stranger which flattereth with her words. (Proverbs 7: 1-5)

23

LET EVERYTHING THAT HATH BREATH PRAISE THE LORD

Hearken unto me now therefore, O ye children, and attend to the words of my mouth. Let not thine heart decline to her ways, go not astray in her paths. For she hath cast down many wounded: yea, many strong men have been slain by her. Her house is the way to hell, going down to the chambers of death. Doth not wisdom cry? and understanding put forth her voice? (Proverbs 7: 24 - 8:1)

HOW TO BE SURROUNDED
BY ANGELS

Why is it, that when we are in trouble, we cry out to the Lord, "Lord, send your angels to come and watch over us and keep us from harm?"

Or we might pray, "Lord, we pray that your angels minister to our needs."

Why would we pray for one or two of his angels to watch over us when we could have a whole multitude of angels surrounding us?

God's throne is surrounded by angels crying "Holy, holy, holy, Lord God Almighty …" (Revelation 4.8).

Why pray for a few angels when, you can be protected by so great a throng of angels?

All we need to do is enter into his presence through worship. Just begin singing praises to God and you will find yourself surrounded by all the angels that are around his throne.

And the four beasts had each of them six wings about him; and they were full of eyes within: and they rest not day and night, saying, Holy, holy, holy, Lord God Almighty, which was, and is, and is to come. (Revelation 4:8)

THE MONKEY TEACHES US HOW TO BE HAPPY

If it makes a monkey happy, then I will try it too!

Steve and I have used this saying for years around our house. We try to eat one banana every day.

I do not know if it helps but it is funny. There are times one of us is grumpy and we remind each other we need to eat more bananas.

Have you ever wished humankind could be more like some of the other creations God made?

The monkey is so carefree and happy, swinging from the trees, content with whatever comes his way.

Humankind seems to be so unhappy sometimes. Why is this? God gave us more to be happy for than any of his other creatures.

We should be rejoicing and jumping with joy over what he has done for us.

What have you allowed to step in and rob your job? Take the time to evaluate your life and replace the things that have caused you be filled with gloom and despair instead of the joy of the Lord.

O taste and see that the LORD is good: blessed is the man that trusteth in him. (Psalm 34:8)

WE ASK TO BE USED BUT WE DON'T WANT TO BE EQUIPPED

I recall many times growing up, I would say, "Jesus use me?" Thinking I could be a missionary, sharing the gospel to some foreign country.

I've always heard if you pray for patience then you will have to go through tribulation. I wasn't praying for patience so I assumed my path wouldn't be one of tribulation.

Expecting the Lord to use me in a great and mighty way without training was impractical.

What commander would send out his soldier to the battle field not knowing what the soldier was to do?

That soldier would immediately be shot down and his body sent back to his homeland in a body bag. The military knows the value of preparing a soldier to understand when to retreat and when to fight. They know to prepare him and his unit for anything that might come against them. The commander understands the value of boot camp.

My Heavenly Father, hearing my prayer, knew that some Spiritual boot camp would be just what I needed. It was the very thing I was resisting but the only thing that would prepare me for what he had chosen for my life.

There have been a lot of bumps and bruises but the training has served me well. It's the battles I've fought and seeing God bring me through them that have strengthened me and made me what I am today.

That he would grant you, according to the riches of his glory, to be strengthened with might by his Spirit in the inner man... (Ephesians 3:16)

27

WHAT PORTRAIT ARE YOU LEAVING BEHIND?

People are watching us every day. They are watching what we do and hearing what we say.

Our children are more likely to do what we do than what we say. Many times we go to the extreme to teach them what we want them to be when they become adults and then, as the teacher, we walk out into the world and do the opposite.

When this happens; the whole slate of what we have taught them is wiped clean. These children see that what we taught them meant nothing in our own personal lives.

My in-laws were not the type of Christians who went on mission trips or even door to door witnessing to others. The things they did do, which spoke louder than anything they ever said, was attend church regularly, read their bible regularly and love the Lord their God faithfully until their last breath.

As the artist in charge of painting your life, what picture are you painting from start to finish?

Are you having to start all over every few years because of the inconsistency of your lifestyle or does your portrait work as building blocks, each year adding more and more color to your work?

When your life is over and people look at the portrait you drew of yourself, what stands out to them?

I am crucified with Christ: nevertheless I live; yet not I, but Christ liveth in me: and the life which I now live in the flesh I live by the faith of the Son of God, who loved me, and gave himself for me. (Galatians 2:20)

ENTANGLED WHALE SHARK IS A REMINDER TO RESCUE THE PERISHING

Have you read the article or seen the video about the whale shark? It was in the waters near Socorro Island, about two hundred fifty miles south of Baja.

The pregnant shark became entangled in a heavy rope. The rope had cut away at its flesh to the point the shark seemed to be giving up the battle for life. There were deep gashes where it appeared that it had wrestled for quite awhile to free itself. Its fins were greatly damaged from this struggle, leading it to give up the fight.

Some local divers as well as many tourists were greatly concerned about the shark's survival. As the divers began to cut the tangled rope, the whale seemed motionless. The instant one of the divers released the ropes from around the fins of the whale shark; its life was renewed and immediately it swam free.

This story reminds me of not just one or two, but millions that have been entangled within the chains of Satan. Are we going to just leave them this way and let Satan suck the life out of them or go to the necessary depths to see that they are set free?

The Spirit of the Lord GOD is upon me; because the LORD hath anointed me to preach good tidings unto the meek; he hath sent me to bind up the brokenhearted, to proclaim liberty to the captives, and the opening of the prison to them that are bound; To proclaim the acceptable year of the LORD, and the day of vengeance of our God; to

29

comfort all that mourn; To appoint unto them that mourn in Zion to give unto them beauty for ashes, the oil of joy for mourning, the garment of praise for the spirit of heaviness; that they might be called trees of righteousness, the planting of the LORD that he might be glorified.

(Isaiah 61:1-3)

Jesus did not just call Isaiah. He is also calling each of us to help free the captives.

May the Lord enlighten our eyes to see those in need of the Savior, in chains of darkness, needing to be set free. [2]

---

[2]http://article.wn.com/view/2012/12/06/Divers_rescued_trapped_whale_sha rk_in_Mexico/

COUNTERFEIT OR REAL?

This is a question asked by many, "Is God real or have we just created this being for everyone to worship?"

If we were to visit the Bureau of Engraving and Printing, we could see money printed that would be crisp and new. There are people who try to counterfeit this money. No matter how hard they try, perfection can't be reached. The counterfeit money is put into circulation and is hard to identify, but an experienced banker can tell the difference.

Have you ever heard of someone trying to counterfeit monopoly money? No, because it's fake. Why would anyone want to counterfeit fake money that has no value?

The same is true with the word of God. Satan knows the word of God is sharper than any two-edged sword. Satan wants to appear to be the real thing and the only way he can come close, is by trying to counterfeit the word of God.

Satan himself proves God's existence by his desire to counterfeit the word of God. Why would Satan try to counterfeit something that isn't real?

If it's hard for us to recognize counterfeit money, why would we think it would be easy to identify a spiritual counterfeit? There is only one way to recognize the difference and that is to read the word of God know it as well as a banker knows real money.

Hast thou not known? hast thou not heard, that the everlasting God, the LORD, the Creator of the ends of the earth, fainteth not, neither is weary? there is no searching of his understanding. He giveth power to the faint; and to them that have no might he increaseth strength.
(Isaiah 40: 28-29)

BEAM ME UP!

Recently while touring a facility with a friend, she made the statement,

"In 30 years I will be sitting on my sofa talking to my grandchildren and one of them will pull out a tiny object that contains the latest technology. This object will be able to beam you up."

"I just know it's going to happen!" she stated.

We laughed and talked about this statement for some time. We never dreamed we would actually live in a day and age that nothing seems impossible. If you can think it up, there seems to be a way to achieve it.

I'm not totally sure when it's going to happen, but in reality we will see that day when people will be beamed up.

I will not be one of the people left behind sitting on the sofa telling my grandchildren that I toured the facility that invented this technology, because I am planning on being one of people that is beamed up!

While we are sitting around trying to figure out how to invent this technology, the Lord, in his great wisdom, is sitting on the throne holding this great knowledge in the palm of his hand. One day he will look down over his great creation and say,

"Are you ready for this?"

I must tell you now that I have special insight on a few things you must do in order to prepare for that day. This knowledge didn't come from touring a facility but comes from the word of God.

LET EVERYTHING THAT HATH BREATH PRAISE THE LORD

There is special clothing that must be worn, a certain place you will need to place your hand and a very specific drink you must have previously consumed in order to be beamed up.

➤ **You will need to be clothed in his righteousness.**

I will greatly rejoice in the LORD, my soul shall be joyful in my God; for he hath clothed me with the garments of salvation, he hath covered me with the robe of righteousness, as a bridegroom decketh himself with ornaments, and as a bride adorneth herself with her jewels. For as the earth bringeth forth her bud, and as the garden causeth the things that are sown in it to spring forth; so the Lord GOD will cause righteousness and praise to spring forth before all the nations.

(Isaiah 61:10)

➤ *Your hand must be placed in the proper spot.*

For I the LORD thy God will hold thy right hand, saying unto thee, Fear not; I will help thee.

(Isaiah 41:13)

➤ *You must drink from the living water*

In the last day, that great day of the feast, Jesus stood and cried, saying, If any man thirst, let him come unto me, and drink. He that believeth on me, as the scripture hath said, out of his belly shall flow rivers of living water.(John 37:38)

➤ *Are you ready for this? Beam me up!*

Then we which are alive and remain shall be caught up together with them in the clouds, to meet the Lord in the air: and so shall we ever be with the Lord. Wherefore comfort one another with these words. But of the times and the seasons, brethren, ye have no need that I write unto you. For yourselves know perfectly that the day of the Lord so cometh as a thief in the night. (I Thessalonians 4:17 – 18:2)

In every thing give thanks:
for this is the will of God
in Christ Jesus concerning you.
I Thessalonians 5:18

WEARING A MASK

None of us wants to admit we are wearing a mask but if the truth be known, we all are. Each person born has a mask on. Since it was placed on us at birth we may not even be aware we have it on.

Adam and Eve were the first people that put on a mask. After Adam and Eve sinned they realized they were naked and made themselves clothing out of leaves. They began to hide from God for the very first time. They have continually passed their mask down to every generation that followed them. The mask they put on was the mask of self-righteousness.

And the LORD God called unto Adam, and said unto him, Where art thou? And he said, I heard thy voice in the garden and I was afraid, because I was naked; and I hid myself. And he said, Who told thee that thou wast naked? Hast thou eaten of the tree, whereof I commanded thee that thou shouldest not eat? And the man said, The woman whom thou gavest to be with me, she gave me of the tree, and I did eat. (Genesis 3:9-12)

Once they sinned, the first thing they did was to hide from God. When God called out for Adam in the garden, Adam hid. The Lord asked him why he hid himself. Adam said, "I was naked and hid myself."

The Lord asked Adam, "Who told you that you were naked?"

Adam immediately said, "The woman whom thou gavest to me, she gave me of the tree, and I did eat." What he was saying is, "Had it not been for her, this never would have happened."

Adam didn't see himself as someone vulnerable to making a mistake.

36

God had walked with Adam every day in the garden. God knew him in a very intimate way. The minute Adam sinned, he immediately reached for the mask. This object became a wall between Adam and God.

Before Adam sinned he was open to God seeing him as he was. The word "intimacy" could be broken down to mean "Into me, see." Once he sinned he was filled with fear, shame and blame. He didn't want the Lord to see him as he was after that point.

Are you wearing a mask to hide from God or are you afraid of the intimacy (into me, see)?

Before Adam and Eve sinned there had been nothing told to them about forgiveness. They had never lived this life before. Then we see the blood of an animal being shed so Adam and Eve could have a covering.

In the Old Testament, we are told of the beginning of blood sacrifices being made. Sacrifices were not to pay for the sins of the people but they were a picture of what was to come. It was pointing to the day Jesus Christ would shed his blood on the cross so we would no longer have to wear the mask. We would be allowed to experience intimacy with the Lord.

And almost all things are by the law purged with blood; and without shedding of blood is no remission.

(Hebrews 9:22)

The Lord is asking you to remove the mask that keeps a wall built up between you and God. By wearing it, you are saying, "Lord, I do not want you to 'into me, see!'"

He already knows what is there but he is waiting patiently for you to remove the mask and admit to him who you really are.

The Lord knew exactly where Adam and Eve were in the garden, yet he called out to them and asked them, "Where are you?" He wanted them to vocalize their need. Once this was done, the Lord met that need.

The Lord is longing and waiting to have a relationship with you but he cannot do it until you remove the mask. It may be one mask that you need to remove or it may be ten.

Some may be wearing the mask of religion. This mask can do as much damage as any of the other ones. This one can give the world a sense that you have intimacy with God, when in fact he isn't able to have a relationship with you because of the rituals and false pretenses you have learned to put on.

You could be at the point in your life that you have removed all the masks but when the Lord says, "Where are you?" there is no response. In order to have that relationship with him, you need to answer his call. Tell him where you are.

When you have removed all the masks, tell him. Tell him you are searching for that intimate relationship with him. Seek the Lord with your whole heart and I promise he will meet you where you are.

For he is our peace, who hath made both one, and hath broken down the middle wall of partition between us; Having abolished in his flesh the enmity, even the law of commandments contained in ordinances; for to make in himself of twain one new man, so making peace; (Ephesians 2:14-15)

WHAT DO YOU WANT TO BE WHEN YOU GROW UP?

Our granddaughter is attending preschool. One day her teachers asked her what she wanted to be when she grows up. She answered, "A church." They asked her several times and each time she responded with the same answer.

Several people have reacted to her statement. One lady said, "Somebody needs to sit her down and explain to her what a church is." I'm thinking to myself, "Lady, somebody needs to sit you down and explain to you what a church is."

A church is not a building in which we meet. It is the people who are members that make up the body of Christ.

Many people have been taught the church building is holy, and we are to show reverence to it- "No running," "Sit still," "No drinks," "Take your hat off," and the list goes on. They will pass this teaching down to their children. These same people will do things to their body that is sinful and think nothing about it.

We should be respectful to the building where we worship but the most important thing to remember is our body is actually the temple of the Holy Spirit. We need to spend each day making sure our body is what we keep clean and pure.

I hope my granddaughter never quits saying she wants to be "a church" when she grows up.

What? Know ye not that your body is the temple of the Holy Ghost which is in you, which ye have of God, and ye are not your own? For ye are bought with a price: therefore glorify God in your body, and in your spirit, which are God's. (I Corinthians 6:19-20)

LESSONS FROM THE MONKEY- LET IT GO

Are you the type person that just can't let things go? It can be something you don't need – anything from clothes, shoes, household items or paperwork.

We can also refuse to let go of bad things. Many times we have unforgiving hearts towards someone. We wait until they say something wrong and then we unload the whole sack of unforgiveness over the top of their heads.

The monkey is a perfect example of how holding onto things can be detrimental. Did you know in some Asian counties they catch monkeys in such a simple way?

To catch a monkey, they cut a small hole in a clay pot or coconut and put a nut inside. The monkey will come along and reach his hand into the container and never let the nut go. He clinches his fist as tight as he can. The only way to set the monkey free is to break the pot or coconut open.

Did you know Satan traps Christians this very same way? We latch onto things that will destroy us. We tighten our grip around it and clinch our fist. No matter who tells us to let go or shows us how to let go, we are not going to. The item is ours and nothing or no one will keep us from having it.

How tight are you holding onto the things that can be detrimental to you? Jesus wants us to experience freedom. You will not truly experience freedom until you let go.

Wherefore seeing we also are compassed about with so great a cloud of witnesses, let us lay aside every weight, and the sin which doth so easily beset us, and let us run with patience the race that is set before us,(Hebrews 12:1)

HIS LOVE FOR ME

Greater love hath no man than this, that a man lay down his life for his friends. (John 15:13)

Today was my last day visiting with my children and grandchildren. I went to church tonight and heard my son preach. My heart was overwhelmed with joy. The love a mother has for her children is unexplainable.

I was thinking about my love for each of my three children and was taken away with the thought that my love is a one percent kind of love. Oh, to me it's one hundred percent kind of love but compared to the love the Lord has for us, it's nothing.

Do your children do everything you reared them to do? Do they stumble and fall? Do they sometimes actually break your heart?

It doesn't matter how many times we have been hurt or worried about them, our love always outweighs the grief or sorrow.

If this is true, how much more does the Father also love you? Once you have confessed your sins and been forgiven, when he looks at you he sees his wonderful beautiful child – the one he longs to spend time with, discuss the future with and just bask with in the moments spent together.

But thou, O Lord, art a God full of compassion, and gracious, long suffering, and plenteous in mercy and truth. (Psalm 86:15)

WHICH FEET TO CHOOSE?

If you were going to start a ministry, who would you choose to be the feet of your ministry? God has shown me not to rely on what I feel but on his desires.

I have a friend who challenged me in the ministry, who has Cerebral Palsy and is in a wheel chair. She told me at the beginning of the "Digging a Well" ministry, that she wanted to be my feet. Many people would have laughed over this statement. I felt lead that God wanted Jonean to be the "feet" of this ministry.

Jonean has been a blessing in my life in so many ways. If Jonean wasn't a part of this ministry, I am positive that it would not exist. When I feel like giving up she urges me on. She believes with all her heart that this ministry is going to help many women become "diggers of faith."

If you were going to choose someone to be the feet of your ministry, would you choose the feet that have been to the beauty salon, perfectly painted, no bunions, wearing the most expensive sandals, or would you choose someone in a wheel chair. Too many times, our choices are based on the outward appearance. This is why so many times we fail in the ministry.

God has shown me he can use people who are disabled in order to glorify him. A blind person is able to see things that we can't, because they rely on their spiritual insight instead of their eyes. A person who is confined to a bed might minister more deeply than those of us who come and go daily as we please.

May God continue to show those of you with disabilities that you can be used in a powerful way for his glory. If you have a disability that has stopped your well from flowing, pray and ask the Lord how he can use your disability for his glory.

THE DOLPHINS TEACH US FAMILY LIVING

When I was young, we lived in Aransas Pass, Texas. One of our favorite pastimes was to ride the ferries across the bay. The highlight of the ferry ride was to see the dolphins swimming and jumping out of the water. Unaware of their protective nature, we were only interested in their beauty.

Then one day, while my father was doing some deep sea construction work, there was a shark swimming toward him! Out of nowhere a dolphin came by and ran the shark off. Learning of this gave us a better understanding about the nature of these beautiful creatures.

Dolphins are family oriented. They run in pods and the pods include males, females, babies and elderly dolphins.

Dolphins are calm and friendly but there are times they get aggressive. One of the times they become aggressive is when something starts to attack one of the elderly or young dolphins. Another example is when a shark tries to attack a human.

The healing process in dolphins is faster than in any of the other mammals. A deep cut from a shark attack heals extremely fast, thus making them less vulnerable.

Most dolphins enjoy socializing and playing. They spend much of their time playing with other dolphins but they will also become playful with other sea creatures and humans as well. Dolphins like to tease and interact with others in a playful manner.

The dolphin has the greatest communication skills of all the sea creatures. They spend most of their time communicating with one another with what seems to be only squeaks and squeals to us.

The dolphin's eyes are connected to two separate areas of its brain. While one section sleeps the other section of the brain is awake and active, watching for predators, making sure nothing sneaks up on the pod.

We need to be like the dolphins and take the time to communicate with, play with, and protect both our younger and older generations from harm.

The scriptures teach us the value of family living. Let's be more like the dolphins and care for our orphans, children and widows. We need to take the time to show them the attention, love and protection they need.

Pure religion and undefiled before God and the Father is this, to visit the fatherless and widows in their affliction, and to keep himself unspotted from the world. (James 2:17)

WHAT DOES YOUR SAIL LOOK LIKE?

Have you ever noticed the sails on a ship? The ship's hull doesn't have a lot of beauty but when the winds pick up and the sails are lifted, the ship takes on a look of majesty. It shows a symbol of strength as the winds become intensified.

What would happen if the fisherman didn't take time to purchase the sails for his ship? What if, when they were torn and destroyed, he went out to sea without repairing them, or he left the anchor lying on the dock thinking it was useless?

The winds would come and the ship would have no protection or guidance. There would be no way to anchor down without the proper equipment. The ship would be tossed around furiously and become broken apart by the fierce winds.

Before you set out on the course of life, be sure and check your sails. Make sure none of them need repaired. You may be like many who don't even have sails for their ships. Before entering the seas of life, take the time and gather the appropriate sails you need in order to face the winds. Take the anchor with you instead of leaving it behind.

Listed below are a few wonderful sails. You can find each of them in the word of God. Take the time to gather what you need for the trip you will be facing. As you are preparing your ship be sure to invite the Lord to come along, for he is the "Master of the Wind" and the "Anchor of your Soul."

➢ Hope - *Lamentations 3:24 The LORD is my portion, saith my soul; therefore will I hope in him.*

➢ Peace - *Colossians 3:15 And let the peace of God rule in your hearts, to the which also ye are called in one body; and be ye thankful.*

➤ Trust - *Proverbs 3:5-6 Trust in the LORD with all thine heart; and lean not unto thine own understanding. In all thy ways acknowledge him, and he shall direct thy paths.*

➤ Patience - *II Thessalonians 3:5 And the Lord direct your hearts into the love of God, and into the patient waiting for Christ.*

➤ Assurance - *John 3:16 For God so loved the world, that he gave his only begotten Son, that whosoever believeth in him should not perish, but have everlasting life.*

➤ Endurance - *Revelation 3:10-11 Because thou hast kept the word of my patience, I also will keep thee from the hour of temptation, which shall come upon all the world, to try them that dwell upon the earth. Behold, I come quickly: hold that fast which thou hast, that no man take thy crown.*

➤ Faith - *Romans 3:22 Even the righteousness of God which is by faith of Jesus Christ unto all and upon all them that believe: for there is no difference:*

It's during the winds that we show the Lord is in control of our ship. These are the times the world sees what we are really made of.

As the winds start to blow, lift the sails to show the majesty of Jesus Christ living in and through you.

As the storms become intense it will be the anchor, the Lord Jesus Christ, which keeps your ship from being toppled and destroyed.

VIEWING THE FUTURE BY OBSERVING THE PAST

Many times I wonder how it would have been to live in the bible days with all the prophecies being fulfilled. Each of the women were waiting with great anticipation to see if they might be the chosen one, the one that would be the mother of the Messiah. Can you imagine being Mary, and hearing the news the angel delivered?

The only way Mary knew what to expect was by viewing the past. She must have started trying to learn all she could about the prophecies of the Messiah. She possibly knew the Savior was to be born of a virgin, born in Bethlehem, and he would save her people from their sins. She must have pondered on how this all was going to take place.

They didn't have the scriptures lying on the coffee table, or data found on an iPhone so she could research and see what was going to take place. Everything she learned was by going to the temple or synagogue and listening intently to what was being taught.

Today we are not waiting to find out who will give birth to the Messiah but there are many things in the scriptures that tell us of things that are coming in the future.

We are waiting for Christ to return for his bride, for the King of Kings to set up his kingdom on this earth. The best way for us to understand what is in the future is for us to observe the past, just as Mary and Joseph did.

The Lord sent prophets to leave tips and hints of events; so we also will wait anxiously for his return. Are you waiting as Mary and the women of the bible did?

God may desire to use you in a mighty way during these days we are in, just as he used Mary to be the mother of Jesus. There are many prophecies left in the bible to be fulfilled. Where do you fit into his great plan?

God, who at sundry times and in divers manners spake in time past unto the fathers by the prophets, Hath in these last days spoken unto us by his Son, whom he hath appointed heir of all things, by whom also he made the worlds; Who being the brightness of his glory, and the express image of his person, and upholding all things by the word of his power, when he had by himself purged our sins, sat down on the right hand of the Majesty on high; Being made so much better than the angels, as he hath by inheritance obtained a more excellent name than they. For unto which of the angels said he at any time, Thou art my Son, this day have I begotten thee? And again, I will be to him a Father, and he shall be to me a Son? And again, when he bringeth in the first begotten into the world, he saith, And let all the angels of God worship him.

(Hebrews 1:1-6)

WHAT WOULD YOUR MOLD LOOK LIKE?

Do you ever look at nature observing the things that have taken place since creation? There are so many wondrous things in the outdoors to behold.

While walking today, I notice a leaf had fallen into some cement and formed a mold. It left an imprint of every line and every curve the leaf had. One could tell everything about the leaf except for the color of it.

As I continued to walk my mind kept thinking back on how awesome it is when people leave the handprint of a small child in the sidewalk. As the child grows into adulthood, he can go back and see that print that was molded decades ago.

I began to wonder how my life would be captured if time stopped today and I was placed into a mold. What would people think my life looked like if they walked by my mold twenty five years from now?"

Would it be one of shame? Would it be one that exemplified dissatisfaction and greed or would it be one of which I could proudly say, "I'm sure glad that is the day my mold was set?"

I have periods of time in my life that I would never want my mold to be made. This gives me reason to press forward toward setting a better mold each day of my life. As we walk each day, let us do our best to leave a wonderful impression for others to view as they pass by.

Search me, O God, and know my heart: try me, and know my thoughts: And see if there be any wicked way in me, and lead me in the way everlasting. (Psalm 139:23-24)

RETRACTION OR REPULSION

There is a group of people that believe the word repent is repulsive. They become angry and defensive if anyone starts singing or speaking about the need to repent.

There is another group of people that would desire to do a retraction. Those are the ones that were repulsed by the word while alive and still able to make that decision but chose not to. Now they are spending an eternity separated from the Lord. They would give anything to be able to hear just one more time that they have the opportunity to repent.

There was a certain rich man, which was clothed in purple and fine linen, and fared sumptuously every day: And there was a certain beggar named Lazarus, which was laid at his gate, full of sores, And desiring to be fed with the crumbs which fell from the rich man's table: moreover the dogs came and licked his sores And it came to pass, that the beggar died, and was carried by the angels into Abraham's bosom: the rich man also died, and was buried; And in hell he lift up his eyes, being in torments, and seeth Abraham afar off, and Lazarus in his bosom. And he cried and said, Father Abraham, have mercy on me, and send Lazarus ,that he may dip the tip of his finger in water, and cool my tongue; for I am tormented in this flame. But Abraham said, Son, remember that thou in thy lifetime receivedst thy good things, and likewise Lazarus evil things: but now he is comforted, and thou art tormented. (Luke 16: 19-25)

Seek the Lord with your whole heart while he still can be found as we see, there comes a day when it's too late.

Seek ye the LORD while he may be found, call ye upon him while he is near: (Isaiah 55:6)

A HEART OF PURSUIT

The Lord is pursuing you. He has done this for quite some time. You were created in His image, to be like him. He has longed to be your Companion, Friend and Comforter.

It is one thing for him to pursue you but it's quite another for you to pursue him.

Have you ever longed to pursue after the Lord?

It can be a life changing experience.

Have you ever been in a relationship where you began to pursue after someone?

There seems to be something missing unless that person shows you interest also. You can dress up, spend time talking with them, and even cook meals for them, while they continue to fail to notice your interest. After some time you might eventually give up.

Jesus Christ took his pursuit for you to the extreme. He didn't ask you to leave your father, he left his. He walked upon the dry dusty earth in order to pave the way for you to have eternal life. He went so far as to die on the cross for you.

Hello! Do you not see what all he has done to pursue a relationship with you?

He isn't like an earthly friend. He doesn't give up and walk away so easily. He has continued to pursue you and wait patiently for you to respond.

You may have longed for this relationship for quite some time not even realizing the very thing you need to do is pursue the Lord.

Take the first step now!

Let's take time out of our daily schedule to begin this pursuit for God.

51

LET EVERYTHING THAT HATH BREATH PRAISE THE LORD

But if from thence thou shalt seek the LORD thy God, thou shalt find him, if thou seek him with all thy heart and with all thy soul. (Deuteronomy 4:29)

The LORD is my light and my salvation;

whom shall I fear?

the LORD is the strength of my life;

of whom shall I be afraid?

When the wicked, even mine enemies and my foes,

came upon me to eat up my flesh,

they stumbled and fell.

Though an host should encamp against me,

my heart shall not fear:

though war should rise against me,

in this will I be confident.

One thing have I desired of the LORD,

that will I seek after;

that I may dwell in the house of the LORD

all the days of my life,

to behold the beauty of the LORD,

and to enquire in his temple.

(Psalm 27: 1-4)

THE STARS TEACH A LESSON IN FAITH

Our little two year old granddaughter is staying the week with us. I have found that she is a visual learner. She also takes most everything literally.

Both my granddaughter and I love to look at the sky outside at night. She will sit and have a conversation with me about the moon and the stars.

When I point to the stars and tell her God made them she agrees. Later while we are still looking at the stars I will ask, "Who made the stars?" She will answer, "God did!"

The next day I will try to reiterate the things we had talked about the night before. Here is how our conversation goes.

"Who made the stars?" She looks at me puzzled and says, "We don't have any."

I explain to her they are there but we can only see them at night. I tell her, "God made the stars!"

Again I say, "Can you tell me who made the stars?" She looks at me seriously and says, "MeeMee, we don't have any!"

I have found if I want to discuss the stars and the moon, it must be done when it's dark and they are visible for her to observe.

Many adults think this same way. There are people serving the Lord with their whole hearts, involved in ministry, that if you ask them, they will tell you they know God is real. They will express how the Lord brought them through many trials.

Later, if you ask that same person about the Lord, they are much like my granddaughter. Instead of saying, "We don't have any" they might say, "He doesn't exist." Just because they

54

can't see him moving visibly in their lives they feel the Lord doesn't even exist.

He might not be shining brightly at that moment in their lives but it doesn't remove the fact that he exists.

If I try to explain to my granddaughter the stars are in the sky but we can't see them because of the sunshine, she isn't going to understand since she is only three. Somewhere down the line she will have to learn to just trust us that the stars are there and they are shining even when we can't see them.

Faith is something all mankind struggles with. It doesn't matter if we are three or eighty years old, there are things we face that cause our faith to waver. There comes a time when people's faith (even of those who have been in the ministry for twenty years) will waver.

There is a story in the bible about a man who had a son that inflicted pain on his own body; there were times the child would throw himself into the water or fire. This had been happening since the child was small. When the father came to Jesus he wanted to believe Jesus could heal him.

Jesus was walking on the earth and could be seen visibly but this father was still having trouble believing. What he did next is what we need to do.

Jesus said unto him, If thou canst believe, all things are possible to him that believeth. And straightway the father of the child cried out, and said with tears, Lord, I believe; help thou mine unbelief. (Mark 9:23-24)

The Lord will help us, but at times we need to admit to him, we are struggling in our faith.

There are other things that will help us also. If my granddaughter did not continue to read and hear about the stars being in the sky during the daytime she would continue to struggle with this fact.

We don't just give up on teaching her this truth. We tell her, books she will read will teach it, and she will hear this truth by people on television or in school. We will teach her in different ways and eventually she will come to the understanding the stars are in fact in the sky during the daytime, even if she can't see them.

So then faith cometh by hearing, and hearing by the word of God. (Romans 10:17)

Just as children need to read and hear about the things they can't see and understand, all of mankind needs to do the same. Faith comes by hearing the word of God. This tells me, if we are lacking faith we need to spend more time in the bible, listening to people teach it, absorbing it anyway we can. We need to ask the Lord to help us believe just as the man who had a son that was out of control.

Now faith is the substance of things hoped for, the evidence of things not seen. (Hebrews 11:1)

WHEN HOPE RUNS DRY

We can make it through life without many things, but one of the things necessary for survival is hope. We can go for a period of time with little hope but when all hope is gone, we can't continue to carry on.

When we place our hope in the wrong things we end up empty handed. It is vital to our emotional, spiritual and physical being that we have a constant supply of hope.

Now faith is the substance of things hoped for, the evidence of things not seen. (Hebrews 11:1)

Continue reading Hebrews eleven and see the people who made it into the hall of faith. Each person listed in this chapter had one thing in common and that was faith. We see in Hebrews, chapter one that faith is the substance of things hoped for. If we lose hope, we tend to lose faith. The scriptures tell us the best way to hold onto that hope.

Let us hold fast the profession of our faith without wavering; (for he is faithful that promised;) And let us consider one another to provoke unto love and to good works: Not forsaking the assembling of ourselves together, as the manner of some is; but exhorting one another: and so much the more, as ye see the day approaching. (Hebrews 10:23-25)

We need a constant renewing and refreshing by gathering together with the people of God and exhorting one another.

If this is an area you are struggling in, take the time to find a Christian friend who can help you and encourage you.

LETTING THE LORD FILL IN THE BLANKS OF YOUR LIFE

There are so many people in our world with great needs. People have medical, physical and emotional needs. God is the only one that can meet those needs. We can be there to hold their hand, cry with them and give words of wisdom. The one thing we can't do is fill in the blanks of their lives.

Each of you has a blank that needs filled in. You can fill in the blank on this paper with what you need in your life. Confess to the Lord what it is and ask him to meet that need.

Lord, my need is: _____.

You are the only one that can change my _____.

You care about me and what this _____ is doing to my life.

I want you to supply everything I am in need of at this time.

I trust you, love you and give you the burden of this _____.

When thou passest through the waters, I will be with thee; and through the rivers, they shall not overflow thee: when thou walkest through the fire, thou shalt not be burned; neither shall the flame kindle upon thee. For I am the LORD thy God, the Holy One of Israel, thy Saviour: I gave Egypt for thy ransom, Ethiopia and Seba for thee. Since thou wast precious in my sight, thou hast been honourable, and I have loved thee: therefore will I give men for thee, and people for thy life. (Isaiah 43:2-4)

58

HOW DO OTHERS SEE YOU WORSHIPING YOUR KING?

How does the world see you worshiping? This is a very touchy subject. We have had many different religions move to the United States over the last ten years and each group worships differently.

The one thing we need to know more than how to worship is – who we need to worship. Who is our King?

The only one worthy of our praise is Jesus. He was born of a virgin, died for our sins, rose again triumphantly and will return again. He is preparing an eternal home for us and will one day return to receive us unto himself. He controls the storms and sets the captives free. He's the healer of sick, broken hearted and defeated souls. He is a friend to the friendless and a father to the fatherless. He gives us hope for tomorrow and joy for our soul.

How do we need to worship him? There are many ways to worship the King. Reading God's word is a form of worship and shows our devotion. The words that come out of our mouths, the songs we sing and the ways we serve others can also be worship.

If people do not see you doing any of these things, then chances are you don't really know the King.

We are not to worship him for show but if we truly love our King it will be displayed in our lives.

He is available at all times and wants to be your constant. Jesus Christ is the only one worthy of your praise.

People are watching everyday how you worship the King.

The Bible says we are to worship the Lord in spirit and in truth. When we believe his word and begin to sing, we enter

59

into worship. It not only affects our life but it affects the lives of people around us. When others see us worshiping our King they will see the importance of true praise – not a superficial praise but a realistic praise that will take them to the throne of God.

True praise is the kind of praise we have when we are with people and when we are not, when things are going good and when they are going bad. It is something that will manifest itself in and through us daily. People can't help but see we love our King.

But the hour cometh, and now is, when the true worshippers shall worship the Father in spirit and in truth: for the Father seeketh such to worship him. God is a Spirit: and they that worship him must worship him in spirit and in truth. The woman saith unto him, I know that Messias cometh, which is called Christ: when he is come, he will tell us all things. Jesus saith unto her, I that speak unto thee am he. And upon this came his disciples, and marvelled that he talked with the woman: yet no man said, What seekest thou? or, Why talkest thou with her? The woman then left her waterpot, and went her way into the city, and saith to the men, Come, see a man, which told me all things that ever I did: is not this the Christ? Then they went out of the city, and came unto him.(John 4:23-30)

FILLING MY LIFE WITH
THE RIGHT THINGS

Have you ever watched a helium balloon rising above the power lines and drifting off into the sky?

If you blow air into a regular balloon it will fall, hit the grass or fence and burst. Fill the balloon with water and the instant you let go, it will hit the ground and burst. When you take the same balloon and fill it with helium it responds in a different way.

Not many substances will allow the balloon to sore high in the sky. Perhaps the safest is a gas called helium. This gas is lighter than air. Since it is so light, when it fills a balloon or blimp they easily rise higher and higher.

It seems to be our human nature to desire to rise above the crowd, climb new heights, and go where no one has ever been. We want to sore with the eagles but how can we when we are hanging with the turkeys?

My life is like this balloon. Filled with all the wrong things, I will not get the results I am looking for. I can fill my life with entertainment and lots of new items but when I lie down at night it's like the balloon hitting the ground. It pops and many times the joy is gone.

The only way to get this kind of temporary, superficial joy back is to keep returning and refilling my life with the same things, entertainment and new items over and over.

Real joy and peace comes, however, when I fill my life with the right things. The Lord desires for me to rise to new heights.

Come unto me, all ye that labour and are heavy laden, and I will give you rest. Take my yoke upon you, and learn of me; for I am meek and lowly in heart: and ye shall find rest unto your souls. For my yoke is easy, and my burden is light. (Matthew 11:28-30)

The scriptures say that if we wait on the Lord and let him be the one that renews our strength, we will "mount up with wings as eagles."

Having learned the importance of filling our lives with the Holy Spirit, now we understand what happens when we're filled with worldliness. We will not desire all the worldly things we once did. Our desires will be to wait until the Holy Spirit passes our way and fills our lives abundantly.

Why settle for second best when you can have the best?

Now the Lord is that Spirit: and where the Spirit of the Lord is, there is liberty. (II Corinthians 3:17)

MERCY AND GRACE SEEN IN THE SAND DOLLAR

There is no creature on the face of the earth that needs more mercy than the sand dollar. The sand dollar is actually slower than a turtle. At least a turtle has a hard shell to protect itself from predators. The sand dollar not only is slow, but delicate. Just the slightest pressure and it breaks.

Have you ever noticed a sand dollar has a star shape in the middle with five slots on the outside?

It's not a coincidence that the number five is displayed twice on the sand dollar. One set of five is on its legs and the other set of five is the slots around the edge.

This little creature's only protection is to bury itself under the sand, clone itself or swallow sand. It will swallow sand to make itself appear larger. The reason it clones itself is so it can split itself and appear smaller to the predator. Many times the predator will leave and look for larger meals.

Is it surprising to you the number five stands for mercy and grace? Looking at the sand dollar we see it is a creature in great need of God's mercy and grace. The five slots on the outside represent mercy and grace.

When we break the sand dollar apart, we will find five skeletons that look like doves. There is one inside of each leg. These dove represents peace.

If we look into the scriptures, we will notice mercy and peace are like two best friends. We see them together many times. Mercy means the kindness and love of God that washes our sins away. Peace means the harmony between two parts, or freedom from any external or internal strife. Nothing slipped past God when he created the world, not even the sand dollar and its delicate make up.

When we come to know Christ as our Savior we must do as the sand dollar, put off the old man. Once the sand dollar splits it is able to produce new parts. We will never be able to put on the new man unless we are willing to put off the old man.

Mercy and peace are the two things we need to have in order to receive grace. First of all, we need the mercy of God to wash our sins away.

Secondly, we will come into harmony with the Lord Jesus Christ. When we are willing to do this then grace is able to walk in and supply us with God's unmerited favor.

That ye put off concerning the former conversation the old man, which is corrupt according to the deceitful lusts; And be renewed in the spirit of your mind; And that ye put on the new man, which after God is created in righteousness and true holiness. Wherefore putting away lying, speak every man truth with his neighbour: for we are members one of another. Be ye angry, and sin not: let not the sun go down upon your wrath: Neither give place to the devil. (Ephesians: 4:22-27)

DON'T BE LIKE THE JELLYFISH!

Don't be like the jellyfish that has no brain, no vertebrae, no central nervous system, and most importantly, no heart. It can only feel by using the loose network of nerves on its outer skin that sends information to a central nerve ring.

The jellyfish spends all of its time floating around in the dark. When it's exposed to light it will retreat back into darkness.

The jellyfish is a beautiful creature when it glows in the dark and is intriguing to watch, much like the beauty in our present day world.

Have you ever tried to get your hands on a piece of that beauty?

This type of beauty will leave you weeping. The sting of a jellyfish can be quite painful or even deadly.

You may be like the jellyfish, pushing away from the light of Jesus Christ. He has shown his light to you through his word and through friends and family. It's just human nature to push away from the light. You may have used hundreds of excuses as to why you can't come to the light of Jesus Christ or why you don't want to come to the light.

The fact still remains; you are in need of the Savior. It's time to quit pushing away from him.

You feel he has ignored you, so you are just doing the same based on your feelings.

You say, "He wasn't there when great trials came my way or when death knocked on my door." His light has always been there. You may have been the one that pushed away from it.

Don't let your feelings be top surface as that of a jellyfish. Trust the Lord with all your heart and let him shine his light of truth on your soul and set you free!

That the God of our Lord Jesus Christ, the Father of glory, may give unto you the spirit of wisdom and revelation in the knowledge of him: The eyes of your understanding being enlightened; that ye may know what is the hope of his calling, and what the riches of the glory of his inheritance in the saints, And what is the exceeding greatness of his power to us-ward who believe, according to the working of his mighty power, Which he wrought in Christ, when he raised him from the dead, and set him at his own right hand in the heavenly places, Far above all principality, and power, and might, and dominion, and every name that is named, not only in this world, but also in that which is to come. (Ephesians 1:17-21)

A DAISY CAN HELP YOU MAKE GOOD DECISIONS

Walking down the back road with two children I was babysitting for the day, one of the girls asked me to do a devotional on a daisy. This flower grows wild all around our alley.

I began to tell her a daisy is a beautiful flower that has a deep brown center and the yellow petal. Each daisy has a small button in the middle called a stigma. We decided that the small button would represent Jesus Christ.

As we hold a daisy in our hands there is a stem with which the flower receives nourishment and the stem represents God. Without God in our lives we wouldn't have nourishment. We wouldn't be able to hold our head up tall and face life.

The button or stigma which represents Jesus Christ is on every one of these flowers. When we took this little button out of the middle of the daisy the petals fell apart. So do our lives fall apart when Jesus is not in the center.

One of the children asked me,

"How do you know when you are choosing right and when you are making the wrong decision?"

Using the flower as the example,

I said, "If someone is leading you toward Christ you know the center of your life is stable and will continue to hold together. If friends, cousins, teachers, television shows, video games, anyone or anything else starts leading us away from Jesus Christ then they will cause the center of the flower to be removed."

When Jesus is no longer the center of our lives we will see the petals start blowing away in the wind.

One day you will find yourself empty and in need of Jesus Christ in your life because of allowing the world to convince you that you no longer need Jesus.

Many times we don't understand enough to cry out to God and ask for him to heal us and take care of us and to restore those petals and we try to keep living our lives without him.

What happens if other things become the center of your life? If money becomes central and the money system fails, then you will have nothing to stand on. If it's your mother or father and they pass away, you will find yourself lost and empty.

Allow Jesus be the center of your flower so all the other areas of your life will stay in place just as the petals on this beautiful daisy. The only way the daisy can stay healthy is because it is drawing nutrients from the stem.

And whatsoever ye do in word or deed, do all in the name of the Lord Jesus, giving thanks to God and the Father by him. (Colossians 3:17)

HOW THE WOODPECKER
TEACHES US TO BE DILIGENT

Have you ever watched a woodpecker hammering his head against a tree?

How can this bird continuously hammer away like this?

A woodpecker[3] might ram his head eight to twelve thousand times against a tree on any given day in order to find food to eat or to build a home for itself.

Hello! I have a headache just thinking about what he does in search of food. My brain gets rattled just having to search through the pantry for something to eat.

The woodpecker hangs onto the tree with his feet. He has two toes that point forward and two that point backwards. He also uses his tail to support himself onto the tree. He is able to hold on in this manner for long periods of time.

The woodpecker will spend hours in search of bugs, seeds, nuts or fruit. It will go to great lengths in order to gather a meal. It constantly hammers away in search of insects or some tree sap buried in the bark in the trees.

What if we were as diligent about finding food for our souls as the woodpecker is about finding one little bug? We would be considered spiritual millionaires. Many people have the word of God lying right before them daily and they never think about picking it up. It would be so easy to feed our souls but instead we choose to fill our lives with unhealthy things.

Let's start being like the woodpecker and going to great

---

[3] http://birding.about.com/od/birdprofiles/a/15-Fun-Facts-About-Woodpeckers.htm

lengths to find the fruit of the spirit; which is love, joy, peace, longsuffering, gentleness, goodness, faith, meekness, and temperance. If we don't, we will just be beating our heads against a wall."

This I say then, Walk in the Spirit, and ye shall not fulfil the lust of the flesh. For the flesh lusteth against the Spirit, and the Spirit against the flesh: and these are contrary the one to the other: so ye cannot do the things that ye would. But if ye be led of the Spirit, ye are not under the law. Now the works of the flesh are manifest, which are these; Adultery, fornication, uncleanness, lasciviousness, Idolatry, witchcraft, hatred, variance, emulations, wrath, strife, seditions, heresies. Envyings, murders, drunkenness, revellings, and such like: of the which I tell you before, as I have also told you in time past, that they which do such things shall not inherit the kingdom of God. But the fruit of the Spirit is love, joy, peace, longsuffering, gentleness, goodness, faith, Meekness, temperance: against such there is no law. And they that are Christ's have crucified the flesh with the affections and lusts. If we live in the Spirit, let us also walk in the Spirit. (Galatians 5:16-25)

ARE YOU GOD?

This is a question my husband has been asked by small children in the ministry.

Wow, what a powerful question! Each of us needs to ask ourselves the question, just to see how it makes us feel. Write down your response on a piece of paper. When I ask myself that question I realize how much I fall short of being all I need to be.

Many of the children in our churches look up to us as being much higher than we could ever obtain. But the truth is still there. They are watching every move we make, everything we say, the clothes we wear, the smile on our faces and how much we love other people.

I had a small child draw a picture of me the other day and it really made me stop and think. Does she really see me like this?

It would be nice if everyone saw me this way. The picture she drew had awkward features but the one thing stood out the most was the smile on my face. When looking at the picture it was the most noticeable thing.

I asked myself, "Do I really smile so much and so big that it would stand out as a feature she would remember?" Is that the first thing other people notice when they see me? If not, this is something to work on.

What do people see when they look at you?

It would be a great thing for every Christian to ask five children to draw a picture of them. The picture will be as they perceive you, as children tend to be honest. The picture of me was from just one child and it makes me wonder what I would get if I received four more pictures.

Some children see us in their minds as wearing a police hat, holding a club in our hand, or being a nurse. We may not have a job doing that but in their minds that is all they see.

Would it not make us examine our lives more closely if we actually thought others saw us as being God?

Would we try to be more loving, helpful and supportive if others looked at us this way?

I beseech you therefore, brethren, by the mercies of God, that ye present your bodies a living sacrifice, holy, acceptable unto God, which is your reasonable service. And be not conformed to this world: but be ye transformed by the renewing of your mind, that ye may prove what is that good, and acceptable, and perfect, will of God. For I say, through the grace given unto me, to every man that is among you, not to think of himself more highly than he ought to think; but to think soberly, according as God hath dealt to every man the measure of faith. (Romans 12:1-3)

WALKING BY FAITH

For five years I drove to another town and worked every day. The drive was sixty minutes there and sixty minutes back home again.

People often asked me why I would do such a thing. My reply was, "That is where God wants me, but I don't know why."

You might ask, "How did you know the Lord wanted you working there if you didn't know why?"

My response would have been, "I don't know."

Many times during the long drives, I questioned if I was really hearing the Lord correctly and doing the right thing or if I had lost my mind. The drive was not always easy.

Upon completing the writing, editing, and submitting of my first book, <u>Digging a Well</u>, I realized why the Lord had placed me in that job.

I was consistently building extremely detailed spreadsheets for the company I worked for there. They were a challenge to build and also a challenge for me to keep up and running.

The last spreadsheet I created would read numbers off of other spreadsheets and then create graphs and charts that were printed weekly and hung on a display wall. The detail of building the spreadsheet and keeping it running was so intense that I watched it constantly, making sure the data was feeding into it correctly.

Little did I realize the deep amount of structure this job had created within my life. I thought I was already an extremely structured person. Never would I need more structure, however, than what it would take to write that book.

The day I completed writing the book and it had been approved I took a deep breath. The first thing out of my mouth was, "If I had not listened to the Lord and continued to make that drive back and forth as I did every day, I could never have completed this book"

For we walk by faith, not by sight: (II Corinthians 5:7)

SHOULD CHRISTIANS "LIGHTEN UP" OR "BRIGHTEN UP?"

I think it's time we "brighten up" instead of "lighten up."

Each time I read posts on the internet or facebook about controversial issues, there is usually a person that will post the comment, "Christians just need to lighten up. There are times that things are drawn, created or posted just to stir Christian emotions." Guess what, it works!

As I read the post I see numerous emotions being expressed openly in both directions. It's not easy to see all the changes in our society and not express our opinions.

Satan would love for Christians to sit down and shut up while he keeps drawing people into his kingdom. He never sits down nor shuts up. He uses movies, songs, games (and the list goes on and on) of things Satan has his stamp on.

Personally, I feel if Christians are silent, then we will only slip further and further into pulling away from God. It's the Christian's voice that needs to be heard, but we need to make sure it is done correctly. If we do it incorrectly, it can do more harm than good.

What we need to do before we speak and share our opinions is to "brighten up" on what the word of God says. When we share our opinion instead of God's opinion, we really do not have ground to stand on.

When we stand on the word of God, then we are standing on truth. That is what will change our world.

Study to shew thyself approved unto God, a workman that needeth not to be ashamed, rightly dividing the word of truth. (II Timothy 2:15)

KNOWING WHICH HAT
TO WEAR

I became a pastor's wife at the age of seventeen, at which time, Steve, my husband, took his first church on an Indian Reservation in Ignacio Colorado.

Steve was the pastor of First Baptist Church in Ignacio which had a mission church to the Southern Ute people. At the age of seventeen, I soon found a pastor's wife must wear many hats or so I thought I needed to.

➤ The first hats I started wearing were of a Sunday School teacher, a Five Day Club leader, Nursery worker, as well as adjusting to having a newborn.

➤ At our second church there were several new hats to wear; Vacation Bible School Director, Pianist, Youth Leader and by this time we had three small children.

➤ At the third church there were even more hats! Hospital Ministry, Fund Raisers, Youth Leader, Vacation Bible School Director, raising my three children and by this time we had taken custody of two teenage girls.

➤ The Fourth church there seemed to be more hats than my closet could hold. Baptist Student Ministries Secretary, Pianist, Vacation Bible School Director, Fund Raisers, Hospital Visits, Youth Leader, and Church Secretary, along with the five children. I soon felt I was switching hats every hour on the hour.

➤ The fifth church slowed down to a Baptist Student Ministry Secretary, Pianist, Hospital Visits, Vacation Bible School Director and back to being the mother of three children.

Twenty five years into our ministry, I was asked to lead a ladies' tea and the Lord placed on my heart to have ladies display all of these hats. I did as the Lord placed on my heart and collected about twelve different styles of hats, thanks to Teena Calley, who graciously provided them for our use.

I gathered all my models up with everything set to go except for one thing. I still didn't have any idea why the Lord had laid the hats on my heart and I didn't know what I was going to say.

It was an awkward feeling knowing I would be speaking and was supposed to have all the ladies model the hats. I knew the Lord wanted me to share all the positions I had filled but the thought kept surfacing, "This will be some useless ladies' tea if that is all I do."

As the days passed I kept praying to the Lord and explaining that I didn't understand. A few days before I was to speak I told the Lord one morning at five a.m. I still do not understand why I am doing this topic. As I opened my bible and started to read Ephesians 6:11 the Lord spoke to my heart and said,

"You have been wearing all those hats that made you look better. The hats that made others notice who you are. Those hats really do not matter. This is the hat I want you to wear, the helmet of salvation!"

I was thinking, "OK Lord, I think I got that one."

It's amazing how the Lord just opens your eyes to the truth of his word in such an amazing fashion.

The Lord knows I am a visual learner so he has to really lay it out there for me. I believe he did on this one.

This hat isn't attractive in any way but it is the hat we need to wear daily.

Put on the whole armor of God, That you may be able to stand against the wiles of the devil (Ephesians 6:11)

And take the helmet of salvation, and the sword of the Spirit, which is the word of God. Praying always with all prayer and supplication in the Spirit, and watching thereunto with all perseverance and supplication for all saints; And for me, that utterance may be given unto me, that I may open my mouth boldly to make known the mystery of the gospel, For which I am an ambassador in bonds: that therein I may speak boldly, as I ought to speak. (Ephesians 6:17-20)

LIFE IS LIKE A PIANO

Our lives are like a piano. As a pianist I have learned the value of the things I do in my life. The choices I make the places I go, and the things I do, are important.

In order for me to play the piano correctly it takes a lot of practice. I wasn't given a natural talent for music and there have been times the Lord and I have had deep discussions about this topic. My heart longs to be able to sit down and play any music put before me, but I'm afraid that just isn't going to happen in my lifetime.

I did learn through some rough years in my life that whatever I put into that piano is what I would get out of it. If I never practiced, I couldn't play. If I practiced a lot, I could play well.

I remember praying and asking the Lord to continually soften my heart, not make me a doormat for others to walk on, but to take the bitterness out of my soul. Each day I would sit and play the piano for hours. I soon found if I was angry I might start out playing angry notes, but as long as it took to soften my heart is how long I stayed at that piano.

My heart was pretty hard and angry so I had to spend hours upon hours each week playing the piano.

After many years of playing the piano every day and talking to the Lord about my deep sorrow and anger, I realized slowly but surely, my heart was healing from all the sorrow and anger.

One day I was sitting at the piano, and a "God thing" happened. You can ask anyone who knows a lot about my piano playing; I do not play by ear. Those who hear me play in public believe I could sit and play just about anything. What they don't know is it takes hours upon hours of practice for me to play one little song. Now, once I play that song, I have it down for the rest of my life.

As I was sitting at the piano one day, the Lord gave me a song. If you were to listen to this piece of music, you probably would say it was written from a person that has extreme peace in their heart.

This would be true but the story and words behind the song is that of great grief, anger, sorrow, suffering and despair. It took me two years of working the evil stuff out of my heart for my fingers to be able to play the song I wrote.

The words began to flow from my mouth and my fingers began to play a soothing piece of music, "Lord I'll Follow You."

We are all going to play a song with our lives whether we want to or not. It can be one of destruction, anger, and despair or one of peace, contentment and joy.

Some of the trials I experienced from 2002-2004 were horrible. Never wanting to recall that experience, but knowing now, had I not gone through this time, I wouldn't have seen the importance of continually digging a well.

There are conflicts we face daily that we have to stop and ask ourselves, "What do I want the ending note of my song to be?"

Know ye not that they which run in a race run all, but one receiveth the prize? So run, that ye may obtain. And every man that striveth for the mastery is temperate in all things. Now they do it to obtain a corruptible crown; but we an incorruptible. I therefore so run, not as uncertainly; so fight I, not as one that beateth the air: But I keep under my body, and bring it into subjection: lest that by any means, when I have preached to others, I myself should be a castaway. (I Corinthians 9:24-27)

HOW TO BUILD CHARACTER

A few weeks ago the pastor of First Baptist Church called and asked me to play the piano for the Baccalaureate. After weeks of practicing Pomp and Circumstance, I am still making mistakes from time to time while playing it.

To me, it is a big thing to make a mistake during the ceremony. "Practice makes perfect so practice we will; practice makes perfect, so we'll practice still." Each time I play, the thought crosses my mind, "What if I make a mistake? Maybe it's time to call them and let them know I can't do it."

This thought kept ringing in my mind all day long. It occurred to me they are relying on me for this. My word was given and there is no reason I can't follow through.

"Oh yes there is! Pride!" Not wanting to humiliate myself in front of a large group would be a good reason to back out.

When there are times I say, "I can't," Nick Vuijicic, a physically challenged individual comes to mind. Nick was born with no arms or legs and is now a motivational speaker. He is not just a motivational speaker but he lives his life in such a way as to not allow his disability to be his excuse for anything.

Now if I had a cast on my arm, then that might be a reason to back out of playing for the Baccalaureate. Maybe if I had been working in the yard and a rock flew up and hit me in the eye then that would be a reason to back out, but to just back out would be a lack of character.

The bad things and hard things are the things that make us better. They are the things that build character in us. Note the word *build*, thus meaning it is going to take time. It's not going to be an easy thing.

If we choose to live in a bubble, we will never learn certain things. This would keep us weak.

81

Just a moment of reflecting on Nick's life helps me get my perspective back in place. If Nick can accomplish all the things he does in life, surely I can play a five minute piece of music in front of a crowd.

If Nick can find happiness and success in life, then why can we not find it?

We are the ones who chose our own path. No matter what you are going though; you can still build character.[4]

I can do all things through Christ which strengtheneth me. (Philippians: 4:13)

---

[4] http://www.youtube.com/watch?v=H8ZuKF3dxCY

O God, thou art my God;
early will I seek thee:
my soul thirsteth for thee,
my flesh longeth for thee
in a dry and thirsty land,
where no water is;
To see thy power and thy glory,
so as I have seen thee
in the sanctuary.
Because thy lovingkindness
is better than life,
my lips shall praise thee.
Thus will I bless thee while I live:
I will lift up my hands in thy name.
My soul shall be satisfied
as with marrow and fatness;
and my mouth shall praise thee
with joyful lips:
When I remember thee upon my bed,
and meditate on thee
in the night watches.
Because thou hast been my help,
therefore in the shadow of thy wings
will I rejoice.
My soul followeth hard after thee:
thy right hand upholdeth me.
(Psalm 63:1-8)

DON'T UNDERESTIMATE
THE POWER OF PRAYER

One of the first ladies' teas I spoke at was held at Calvary Baptist Church in Andrews, Texas. I was living in Burkburnett, Texas at the time. Ladies ministry was the last thing in my mind.

My baby sister, Kay Rowe lived in Andrews and attended that church. She was to organize a ladies' tea that would be held at their church. The Lord had been dealing with my heart for months about the twenty-seventh Psalm. Verse four of this chapter had been my life verse, but the Lord was showing me how the whole twenty-seventh Psalm would be my life chapter.

Kay called me one evening and asked if I would be the speaker at the ladies' tea. My response was a quick, "no!" I had never spoken in front of people and I was not planning on starting. Fear beyond anything you can imagine crept through my body at the thought.

Kay sat quietly for a moment and then asked, "If God wanted you to speak to the ladies, what would you speak on?" She set me up and I had no idea until later. I took a deep breath and said, "If I were to speak, it would be on the twenty-seventh Psalm," knowing all the time the Lord would never ask me to do such a thing.

Kay told me the date she had the ladies' meeting scheduled and asked me to pray about it. Since, at the time, I was busy helping the Baptist Student Ministries with an event, it would have been easy to get out of speaking at the tea.

Do you think that stopped my sister? No, because she had prayed with a group of ladies and they felt I was the one that should come.

She gently said, "Why don't you ask your director if there is any way you can be excused?" I knew I couldn't be excused, so it was no sweat off my back.

The next day, I entered into my boss' office and asked him the big question, "Would it be possible to miss the event we had scheduled?"

After popping the question and feeling confident of what his response would be, my boss informed me the event had been called off due to unforeseen issues.

"No, this could not be happening!"

This really disturbed me. With great reluctance I called Kay and let her know I would be the guest speaker. Little did I know, the Lord was wrapping his arms around that whole event and was going to do a great thing.

While speaking on Psalm twenty-seven, a lady that was attending began to weep. The more I spoke the more she wept. When the meeting dismissed, this lady waited to speak with me. She had a bracelet in her hand. As she placed it into my hands, she shared her prayer.

She had prayed much for a young woman. Many years ago, when the young woman was still just a girl, she was working at the older woman's house. On one of the days the girl worked for her, the girl's mother took her own life herself.

She had kept track of this young lady for many years, without the child knowing. She had prayed for her often, that she would grow to be a godly woman. Many years passed, the girl married, moved to Houston, and she had lost track of her.

The woman standing beside me had continued to pray for this girl. She had begun to ask the Lord to open the door where she could once again find this person and see if God had answered her prayers.

As I was speaking, she realized that her secret sister, Kay Rowe, was the woman she had been praying to find. She put my testimony together and knowing Kay was my sister, she realized why the Lord had put on their hearts to have me come speak. Her prayers for the child had been answered.

This was the beginning of seeing how God could use my obedience to him to help others.

My topic wasn't one that would blow anyone away. It was not one full of laughter. The words I spoke that day were from my heart and the Lord used them in a mighty way, not only in this lady's life, but also in mine. He showed me that day the power of obedience.

As I write this devotional, I have the bracelet lying beside me. Oh! I marvel at the wonder of my God!

Ask, and it shall be given you; seek, and ye shall find; knock, and it shall be opened unto you: (Matthew 7:7)

CLIMBING ABOVE THE CLOUDS

Do you struggle with depression? Do the clouds seem too heavy above you at times?

Flying home from Garland on Thursday, I noticed the sky was covered with clouds above us. Some of the clouds looked like giant mountains. For some time we traveled under the clouds and then the pilot decided it was time to get above the clouds. You could tell when his decision was made. He set his guages, geared the plane up, set the nose of the plane in an upward direction and before we knew it, we were cutting though the massive clouds. There was turbulence but the pilot didn't give up and turn the nose of the plane downward to get out of the turbulence; he kept moving upward. Slowly the clouds began to fade, the sky became bright blue and as I looked out the window the clouds now looked like a beautiful ocean underneath us.

I have noticed in my life, when I get depressed I stay there for a period of time. One of the reasons I just stay there is because I don't take the necessary steps in order to rise above it. I might gear up but I forget to set the gauges correctly, I may set the gears but forget to hold my head up high. You see, it also takes some effort on my part to climb above the clouds. I learned several years back that the direction I set my head and shoulders will determine my outlook on life. If I am defeated, my shoulders sag and my head is dropped. If I have confidence, my shoulders are squared and my head set in the direction I am going.

My need is to trust my co-pilot, Jesus Christ, to remind me of all the things necessary to climb above the clouds. I must be willing to hear his voice, follow his wisdom and read the manual, God's Word, daily in order to set my course and stick to it.

All three steps must be done in order to climb above the clouds.

Be prepared for turbulence. I have never tried to climb above the clouds without having turbulence. There is always someone or something that comes against me during the process. Keep moving forward, never changing your direction, knowing after passing through the turbulence that you will soon find yourself above the clouds.

The LORD is my shepherd; I shall not want. He maketh me to lie down in green pastures: he leadeth me beside the still waters. He restoreth my soul: he leadeth me in the paths of righteousness for his name's sake. Yea, though I walk through the valley of the shadow of death, I will fear no evil: for thou art with me; thy rod and thy staff they comfort me. Thou preparest a table before me in the presence of mine enemies thou anointest my head with oil; my cup runneth over. Surely goodness and mercy shall follow me all the days of my life: and I will dwell in the house of the LORD for ever. (Psalms 23:1-6)

BFF– BEST FRIENDS FOREVER

A trip to see my three children and grandchildren was the highlight of my week. You just can't understand how much love parents have in their heart for their children until you are one.

Take as much love as a parent has in their heart for their own child and times that by two. That is what it is like to have grandchildren. I have always heard just how wonderful it is, but until you experience it for yourself, you really don't understand what others mean. It is just an awesome feeling to know your child was able to produce something so sweet, loving and adorable and it's part of you also.

We were able to stay four days in Garland with our children. Our granddaughter and I would play each day as if it were going to be our last. We would swing, go walking, collect leaves, pretend to cook, watch Veggie Tales and we can't forget to do bubbles each day. We go swimming and shopping, turn flips and do silly fun songs. The whole trip is packed with MeeMee and her little giggles.

As we played on Thursday morning, she informed me, "Sadie is my friend! Izzy is my friend! MeeMee is my friend!"

I understood right then and there she loved, loved, loved her MeeMee. When she says you are her friend that means she loves you with every part of her being and she wants to be with you all the time. My heart swelled with pride because of all the wonderful people she knows and plays with, I was listed as one of her three friends.

Each time we visited she would tell me Sadie and Izzy were her friends, but this time I was included.

Thursday evening we loaded our bags and headed to the airport to fly back to good old West Texas. Everything on the trip was fun and games until MeeMee had to tell her best friend forever, goodbye. My granddaughter hugged me so tight and cried her little eyes out saying, "No, MeeMee! No MeeMee!" My heart just broke having to leave her.

Do you ever wonder if this is what the Lord feels when we walk away from him?

He took the time to not only say we are his best friend forever but he loved us so much he purchased us so we could be together all the time. We are his favorite BFF and then for us to walk away from him almost seems heartless.

What exactly does he feel?

Does he grieve when we leave?

Are you willing to give up something in order to have a relationship with a person?

Your BFF was willing to give up his only Son so he could have a relationship with us. The sad part is, we still walk away from him. It's not that we are required to walk away; it's just that we don't understand the depth of his love and how much it breaks his heart.

As the Father hath loved me, so have I loved you: continue ye in my love. If ye keep my commandments, ye shall abide in my love; even as I have kept my Father's commandments, and abide in his love. These things have I spoken unto you, that my joy might remain in you, and that your joy might be full. (John 15: 9-11)

DO YOU HAVE TROUBLE
BEING A GLOVE?

We are all a glove whether we want to be or not. I will be honest with you; there have been times I wanted to hang a sign out that said, "GLOVE NOT IN USE." We will never be able to do that because every day we use our hands for good or for bad.

Each morning when we rise, we need to ask the Lord to let us be the glove in which he places his hand. When we do, we are giving up our will to the Lord and allowing him to have control. It will not be what we want to do that day but what the Lord would have us do. If we do not ask the Lord to wear the glove then we will be allowing someone else to wear the glove.

Have you ever allowed bitterness to slide its hand into your glove? As you go through the day and begin to dwell on the thing that caused you bitterness, you attack someone or something and cause destruction. The reason we do this is because we allow bitterness to wear the glove that day.

Have you ever allowed hatred to slide its hand into your glove?

Daily, we read or hear news of people committing horrendous, hateful crimes like murder and child abuse. What if they had awakened that morning and allowed the Lord to wear the glove that day rather than hatred. Not only would these lives be saved, but also the agony of the person that wore the glove would have been prevented.

What about the glove of rejection?

This glove allows the hand to go right out in front of the person as if to say, "Oh no, buddy, don't you think you will be crossing that line," or "Talk to the hand because the face don't understand."

Many times we feel we have the right to wear this glove. When we allow rejection to slide its hand into our glove, we aren't just hurting the people who have hurt us, but we also hurt innocent bystanders.

What about yourself? Have you ever worn the glove of rejection only to realize the glove didn't fit? The glove was so tight it ended up wounding you far more than it did the other person.

Put on therefore, as the elect of God, holy and beloved, bowels of mercies, kindness, humbleness of mind, meekness, longsuffering; Forbearing one another, and forgiving one another, if any man have a quarrel against any :even as Christ forgave you, so also do ye. And above all these things put on charity, which is the bond of perfectness. (Colossians 3:12-14)

MY LIFE IS LIKE A TELEVISION, MY HEART THE REMOTE CONTROL

My life is like a television and each day I have a choice of which channel I will set my life on. My heart is the remote control and I am the only one that can change the channel. This makes me realize just how great of a responsibility I have to the world around me.

And if it seem evil unto you to serve the LORD, choose you this day whom ye will serve; whether the gods which your fathers served that were on the other side of the flood or the gods of the Amorites, in whose land ye dwell: but as for me and my house, we will serve the LORD. (Joshua 24:15)

The first station we should turn on in the morning is the Lord. We are the ones in control of the remote. When people come into our lives during the day and try to change our attitude by planting anger, fear, doubt and worry, we are given a choice.

But seek ye first the kingdom of God, and his righteousness; and all these things shall be added unto you. (Matthew 6:33)

I can leave my heart on the channel I set it on to begin my day with, or I can change the channel. I might say, "At work today Johnny made me so angry."

This really is not a correct statement. What really took place was, at work Johnny said something and my mind began to process the thought. Johnny wasn't the one who changed my channel. I was given a choice of which direction to go. If I allowed anger to creep into my heart then I was the one that changed the channel. I should have taken responsibility, because I was the one that brought the anger upon my own self.

When I heard Johnny's words, I began to process the thought. I could choose to be angry with Johnny or to forgive Johnny. I also could talk to Johnny and see if I misunderstood what he was actually saying. If I chose to change the channel and let anger be what shows on my television then that is what the world would see.

Finally, brethren, whatsoever things are true, whatsoever things are honest, whatsoever things are just, whatsoever things are pure, whatsoever things are lovely, whatsoever things are of good report; if there be any virtue, and if there be any praise, think on these things. Those things, which ye have both learned, and received, and heard, and seen in me, do: and the God of peace shall be with you. (Philippians 4:8-9)

Keep thy heart with all diligence; for out of it are the issues of life. (Proverbs 4.23)

THE PIÑATA REVEALS
THE TRUTH

This week I was babysitting several children. We spent several days making a piñata. Therefore, it doesn't surprise me that it was one of the topics chosen for a devotion by one of the girls.

I showed them that the first step to building a piñata is to blow a balloon up. This balloon represents our heart. It is soft and pliable. The balloon will drift in the direction you blow it and when our heart is soft the same is true. When the Holy Spirit moves in our lives then we are willing to go where he tells us.

Each day the children and I would mix flour and water to make a paste. We would soak a piece of newspaper in the flour and water until it was gummy. One piece at a time, we would place the newspaper strips onto the balloon.

The newspaper tells us of all the things in this world and how we allow other people to influence us. We could even find ourselves doing some of the things written on those pages.

At first the balloon was still soft and pliable. The next day we would go through the same process of dipping the newspaper into the gummy flour and adding it to the balloon.

The second day the balloon was still soft and pliable.

The third day we added another layer of wet gummy newspapers to the balloon and set it outside to dry.

The fourth day, we walked outside and suddenly we could see a change in our pliable balloon. It was no longer soft. The balloon was now hard. It was amazing how hard it had become. When we hit it with our hands it actually hurt our hand.

The balloon that once was easily directed with just our breath had now become impossible to move when we blew air upon it.

As we are going through life, we need to make sure we do not allow people to put all the filth from the world into our hearts.

We may not even realize our hearts are becoming harder and harder every time we allow worldly things to enter in.

One day we will wake up and realize we have allowed ourselves to be hardened. When the Lord tries to speak to us, we can't even hear him. There is only one way to get our heart back to where it needs to be.

A new heart also will I give you, and a new spirit will I put within you: and I will take away the stony heart out of your flesh, and I will give you an heart of flesh. And I will put my spirit within you, and cause you to walk in my statutes, and ye shall keep my judgments, and do them. And ye shall dwell in the land that I gave to your fathers; and ye shall be my people, and I will be your God .I will also save you from all your uncleanness: and I will call for the corn, and will increase it, and lay no famine upon you.

(Ezekiel 36:26-29)

WHAT DO YOU PICK UP WHEN YOU ARE OUT IN THE WORLD?

Behind our house is a field covered in cacti, tumbleweeds and stickers of several kinds. As I was out searching for grasshoppers, there were things that found me before I found the grasshoppers. I searched for twenty minutes only to catch one grasshopper for the praying mantis I have in a cage. The praying mantis was borrowed so I could do an object lesson on Sunday.

I noticed during my search, my life was being affected by the objects all around me. When I finished and entered the back door of our house I was carrying more than a grasshopper. My sneakers had accumulated nine stickers. My pants leg had tumbleweed splinters stuck to them and there were a couple of cockleburs clinging to me.

I was expecting to come in the house with one object but had accumulated lots of unwanted items in the process. These nuisances brought pain when I tried to remove them but I knew it was better to remove them than to leave them and be wounded worse by them later on.

When we enter our world each day, the same thing is going to happen in our spiritual life. We may be searching the internet for something godly and instead a popup shows up in front of our face. This popup might be one that provokes ungodliness. We have the choice to sit and leave it on or remove it. The choice to leave it may be one that brings deep sorrow and wounds later on down the line. The best thing to do is destroy it right then and there.

Abhor that which is evil; cleave to that which is good. (Romans 12:9)

There are other things that tend to latch themselves onto us. Foul language is something we are hearing more and more of. Sometimes when we hear these words, we tend to use them ourselves. It surprises me at the amount of parents that latch on to foul language and use it in front of their small children. Later on the parent may smack the child if they ever use the word.

Be careful when you go out into the world. Make sure you are not bringing things back into your home that will bring pain, confusion and suffering.

Let no corrupt communication proceed out of your mouth, but that which is good to the use of edifying, that it may minister grace unto the hearers. And grieve not the holy Spirit of God, whereby ye are sealed unto the day of redemption. Let all bitterness, and wrath, and anger, and clamour, and evil speaking, be put away from you, with all malice: And be ye kind one to another, tenderhearted, forgiving one another, even as God for Christ's sake hath forgiven you. (Ephesians 4:29-32)

DIVING BOARDS SHOW US OUR NEED TO GO DEEPER

Do you ever feel the need to rise above your problems? A springboard enables you to rise higher and then plunge into deeper depths. So what is holding you back? Let's dive in and explore the treasures from beneath.

Hope can be a spring board. I have found this to be true in my own life. If there is no hope, I will not desire to dive in. If my future looks bleak, with no excitement, I'm not as likely to use this springboard to help me plunge deeper. It can be right in front of me but if I don't use it, it will never change my view.

Once the springboard of hope is put to use, you will rise above your problems and be on your way to diving into the truth. When you enter these waters, life will begin to take on a new dimension. Diving into the truth will help you reach the Father's heart and see the depths of his wondrous power in your life.

Happy is he that hath the God of Jacob for his help, whose hope *is in the LORD his God: which made heaven, and earth, the sea, and all that therein is: which keepeth truth for ever: Which executeth judgment for the oppressed: which giveth food to the hungry. The LORD looseth the prisoners: The LORD openeth the eyes of the blind: the LORD raiseth them that are bowed down: the LORD loveth the righteous: The LORD preserveth the strangers; he relieveth the fatherless and widow: but the way of the wicked he turneth upside down. The LORD shall reign for ever, even thy God, O Zion, unto all generations. Praise ye the Lord. (Psalm 146:5-10)*

FEED MY SHEEP

We lived in Ignacio, Colorado during the early years of our ministry. There was a couple in our church that my children loved and adored. Glenn and Jeannie Faverino took us under their wing and it didn't take long before our children started calling them Uncle Glenn and Aunt Jeannie.

When Josh was three years old he would follow Glenn around everywhere. We spent quite a bit of time on their ranch in Arboles, Colorado. Steve and Josh would go outside with Glenn and feed the horses while Jeannie and I prepared the meals. We were unaware that Josh was watching intently every move Glenn made.

Josh soon gained a love for horses that was manifested on a daily basis. He owned his own horse and had an area in his backyard sectioned off, so his horse couldn't escape. Josh made sure his plastic bouncing horse was well taken care of each day.

Each morning after breakfast, Josh would inform me he was headed out to feed the horse. He would gather his pail, fill it with sand and carry it over to the horse. He would stand there for quite some time making sure his horse had been given plenty to eat.

Josh performed this daily ritual every day. After making sure his horse had been fed and taken care of, he then would go for a ride. Josh learned the need to take care of his horse by watching Glenn. We never had to show him how to carry this task out. He learned it by seeing it demonstrated.

In John chapter twenty-one, this was the third time Jesus appeared to his disciples after his crucifixion. The Lord knew he would shortly ascend to His Father. He wanted to make sure his children would be taken care of. He wanted to be sure that

Peter and the disciples had been watching him intently and knew what to do once he ascended to the father.

When our children lived at home and we planned to leave, I wanted to make sure they were in safe hands. Not just the hands of a person who would sit in the house and be available, but someone that would watch them intently. I wanted to be sure that person would take care of *all* their needs; needs for protection, food, bathing and then place them into bed with care.

The Lord, at this point, is making sure Peter will not only feed his sheep but he is probing into the depths of Peter's heart. He desired to see if Peter was willing to do everything needed for his children's safety and maturity during his absence. He didn't only probe Peter to see how well he would feed his sheep; he also probed to see if Peter was willing to care deeply for his lambs.

The Lord is about to hand over the Keys to the Kingdom to Peter. He is expecting Peter to keep the gospel alive and to pass it on to others. It wasn't just for one generation of sheep but for many generations to come.

We see each time Jesus asked Peter this question, there was more depth. He probed him to the point it frustrated Peter. But when it was all said and done, the Lord knew Peter was the one to receive the Keys to the Kingdom. He knew the depths of his love.

How much do you love him? The Lord may be asking you at this point, "_____, will you feed my sheep?" What will be your response?

There have been many faithful witnesses that have gone before us. Let us learn from the footprints they left behind how to take care of the Lord's sheep.

This is now the third time that Jesus shewed himself to his disciples, after that he was risen from the dead. So when they had dined, Jesus saith to Simon Peter, Simon, son of Jonas, lovest thou me more than these? He saith unto him, Yea, Lord; thou knowest that I love thee. He saith unto him, Feed my lambs. He saith to him again the second time, Simon, son of Jonas, lovest thou me? He saith unto him, Yea, Lord; thou knowest that I love thee. He saith unto him, Feed my sheep. He saith unto him the third time, Simon, son of Jonas, lovest thou me? Peter was grieved because he said unto him the third time, Lovest thou me? And he said unto him, Lord, thou knowest all things; thou knowest that I love thee. Jesus saith unto him, Feed my sheep.

(John 21:14-17)

A PENCIL SHOWS THE NEED TO BE FILLED WITH THE SPIRIT

Writing on my blog has become my passion. It has become such a part of me that I am now dreaming about writing. I tried one day not to write at all – to just take a day off. It just didn't happen. I had gone four hours into the day and a topic was on my mind to the point it was going to drive me crazy if I didn't stop and put it onto paper.

I dreamed last night I was a pencil. Seriously, it was quite funny. I dreamed it was time to write and there was no lead inside of me. This was frustrating to me that I was unable to write what I wanted to write. I was unable to accomplish my task due to my neglect to refill the pencil.

Have you ever picked up a pencil and started to write only to find out there was no lead inside? Someone had failed to refill the compartment, leaving you with nothing to write with. It is impossible to complete your project until you get up, search the drawers, find the lead and place it into the cylinder of the pencil. Once the cylinder holds the lead, you will be able to start writing.

Our lives are much like this lead pencil. If we decide to be used of God and we haven't been filled with him, nothing will come out. You may become frustrated, but the truth is, you never searched for nor opened the cylinder of your life and allowed your Father to fill it.

Until you realize your life is empty, you probably will not realize the need to be filled. Don't wait until it's time to be used to find out you haven't let the Father fill you with the Holy Spirit.

You may be like the pencil and you have given yourself to the Lord. You can be saved, yet not filled with the Holy Spirit. Have you allowed your vessel to sit there and not be filled?

How many times do we do this very thing? The Lord is waiting to fill your vessel. He may be waiting for you to get up, look for his indwelling, and ask him to place his word into your life so you can be filled. In doing so, you will be able to be used of him.

Whatever I allow my pencil to be filled with is what will come out when I begin to write. Therefore, if I don't want a mess and I want my words to be precise and able to be read by others, it is vital I fill that pencil with lead.

"Filled," means to put an item into the vessel to the point it is about to run over if you put in more. As we see in the verse below there needs to be nothing else in the vessel – only him.

And be not drunk with wine, wherein is excess; but be filled with the Spirit; Speaking to yourselves in psalms and hymns and spiritual songs, singing and making melody in your heart to the Lord; Giving thanks always for all things unto God and the Father in the name of our Lord Jesus Christ; Submitting yourselves one to another in the fear of God. (Ephesians 5:18-21)

CARRY THE LIGHT

As a child I remember going to my grandmother's house in Alabama. If someone asked where she lived, we would say, "The Holler." It seemed like it took forever to get down into that old holler. There always seemed to be some wide open space in the fields until you turned down Mary Davis Holler Road, the last road that led to MawMaw Poss' house. Here, the trees engulfed the road, making it extremely dark at night but enchanting during the daytime.

If it was daytime when we arrived, the six of us children loved to visit the hill behind MawMaw's house. We used to think this hill was the tallest one in all the area. As we go back and visit now, we are amazed to see how small the hill actually is.

If it was nighttime when we arrived, I remember the excitement of catching fireflies. We lived in a part of Texas where there were no fireflies, thus making it wondrous fun to visit the holler. These little critters were numerous back in the woods. We would chase them and put them into jars. I know this was cruel but we smeared the bottom half of the firefly onto our clothing so they would glow in the dark.

These fireflies are becoming extinct. There may come a day when their light is no longer able to be seen. This reminds me of a quote from Ronald Reagan, "Freedom is never more than one generation away from extinction. We didn't pass it to our children in the bloodstream. It must be fought for, protected, and handed on for them to do the same, or one day we will spend our sunset years telling our children what it was once like in the United States where men were free."

The freedom in the United States gives you the privilege of sharing your light with the world. You now have the freedom

105

to share the gospel with any and everyone you choose. Are you doing everything possible to keep our freedom? People shed their blood so we could be free. Are you willing to let them die for no cause or will you take a stand with them and help America protect its freedom?

Jesus Christ has done the same for us. His blood was shed so you and I might live. Was his blood shed in vain? Is the price he paid for you just going to be thrown away, disregarded or ignored?

He holds the key. All you have to do is accept it and you can walk in freedom.

"We the People" need to stand for our freedom in America so we will be able to carry the light to the next generation. We need to make sure this is not the generation that drops the baton. The generation following ours needs to hear the saving gospel of Jesus Christ. Are you willing to run the race and make sure they get that opportunity?

And ye shall know the truth, and the truth shall make you free. (John 8:32)

Being then made free from sin, ye became the servants of righteousness. (Romans 6:18)

Stand fast therefore in the liberty wherewith Christ hath made us free, and be not entangled again with the yoke of bondage. (Galatians 5:1)

ACORNS SHOW US THE NEED
TO SOW MANY SEEDS

Yesterday I was outside sweeping the sidewalk. We have several oak trees in our yard. As I was sweeping, I was astonished at how many acorns there were. They had fallen into our yard, driveway and even over into our neighbor's driveway.

These acorns falling have produced hundreds of little oak trees sprouting up in our yard. There are so many sprouts that the grass has decided not to grow in that spot any longer.

As I continued to sweep I realized there weren't hundreds of acorns that fell to the ground and produced hundreds of oak tree sprouts. There were thousands of acorns that fell from the tree. They produced hundreds of oak tree sprouts.

Jesus tells us we are to bring forth much fruit. You might be like me and ask, "How can this be done when I live in such a rural area?" Another question you may ask is, "How can you use me with my talents and abilities being so limited?"

First we need to know what the seed is and if it's able to produce fruit. In Luke 8:11 the scripture says, "The seed is the word of God." I don't know about your bible but mine is full of scriptures or should I say, "Seed." So our next question is, "Why are you not scattering the seed?"

You may find yourself in the same spot as I did four years ago. When we moved to this town, I told the Lord he had brought me twenty miles the other side of the earth to a place that seems impossible for me to carry out his calling.

I remember one day praying and telling the Lord I was tired of living in small places and producing small fruit. I specifically said out loud to my Father, "It's about time you produce much fruit in and through me and I don't see how you are going to do it in Kermit, Texas."

What a statement. The scripture says in Matthew thirteen, "The mustard seed is the least: but when it is grown, it is the greatest among herbs, and becomes a tree, so the birds of the air come and lodge in the branches thereof." The Lord can use little old me, in little old Kermit to spread his seed if I but pick the seed up and start sharing it.

The ministry where we live now has been the greatest ministry we have had in the thirty-two years we have served. We have given out more bibles, used the blog as a way to minister, and seen more people saved in Kermit than anywhere else. Why have we seen this take place? Was it because I became frustrated? No, the only reason we have seen fruit in this ministry is there has been many seeds planted.

As with the acorns in my front yard, there were thousands that fell, but only hundreds reached fertile soil? This is a perfect example that we need to be about our Father's business of scatting the seed, his word, to the lost world.

Pray and ask the Lord how he can use you. He has used me in ways I never expected since I shared my heart with him. What is he waiting to do in your life if you but trust him? He is only asking you to scatter the seed; let him do the rest.

For the word of God is quick, and powerful, and sharper than any twoedged sword, piercing even to the dividing asunder of soul and spirit, and of the joints and marrow, and is a discerner of the thoughts and intents of the heart. (Hebrews 4:12)

K'NEX USED TO
SHOW TEAM PLAY

This last week we had a group of boys that have had a difficult time getting along with each other at school and at church. Needing some good games to help them learn to get along with each other, I began to search the Internet.

Before leaving the house I organized all the items needed to play the games I had studied out on my computer. Walking into my garage, before entering my vehicle, my eye caught the box of K'NEX that sat on a shelf. These K'NEX used to belong to my boys during their younger years. I'm not sure what possessed me to pick the box up but I quickly tossed it into the back seat.

Upon beginning the class it didn't take long to realize the wonderful games I had pulled off the Internet were not going to be the key I was looking for. These boys needed something different. I love it when the Lord does this. I plan a lesson out and he shows up and takes over.

Instead of following through with my plans I had to trust the Lord that he knew best. I placed the boys about two feet apart and opened the box of K'nex.

➢ Boy # 1 received all wheels.

➢ Boy # 2 received all five inch sticks

➢ Boy # 3 received all clips

➢ Boy # 4 received all one inch sticks.

Each boy was asked to take his own items and build something. As you can see, this was impossible. They soon became frustrated and this was my golden opportunity. Suddenly they realized that by themselves they were nothing.

At this point the real game began. The main rule of the game was to communicate with the other boys. They had to say the boy's name and then ask for a piece of equipment that was in their possession. They were not allowed to receive the object unless they specifically said the boy's name and the other boy gave them permission.

Before leaving the church last night these four boys had constructed a car. They were laughing and enjoying each other instead of verbally and physically attacking one another.

Is this what our Father wants us to learn to do as fellow Christians? We are able to accomplish so much more when we work together. When we treat others with kindness, the Psalmist said, "It is like precious ointment upon the head."

There are times we don't even know why we are not getting along. We just get in the habit of being unwilling to take the time to say the person's name and communicate with them.

Go ahead and try pouring some of the precious ointment on those that seem to be your enemy. You never know what the Lord will do when you start working together. It is through our working together that we are able to reach more for Christ.

Behold, how good and how pleasant it is for brethren to dwell together in unity! It is like the precious ointment upon the head, that ran down upon the beard, even Aaron's beard: that went down to the skirts of his garments; As the dew of Hermon, and as the dew that descended upon the mountains of Zion: for there the LORD commanded the blessing, even life for evermore. (Psalm 133:1-3)

PRAYING MANTISES SHOW OUR NEED FOR NEW GROWTH

Do you ever wake up sometimes and feel there is something in your life that needs to be removed? This is something we all go through. There are things we allow in our lives that drag us down. The question is, "Are you going to allow it to stay or will you get rid of it?"

Have you ever noticed a praying mantis? The instinct placed inside these little critters is amazing. Their instinct tells them in order to grow there is something they will have to do. They will have to put off the old in order for new things to take place in their lives.

Did you know the praying mantis is the only insect that can turn his head freely all the way around? It isn't like the rest of the insects. We need to realize we are not like the rest of the world. We have the ability to turn our heads and make sure our eyes are set on the things of the Lord.

Mankind was not created with just instinct but with intelligence also. It would do us good to learn from God's creation and his word, the things we need to do in our own lives.

Paul tells us in Ephesians we need to put off the former things in our lives. The only way to put on the new and move forward in our Christian lives is to put off the old.

Putting off the old is something the praying mantis does repeatedly during his lifetime. His instinct lets him know when it's time to grow. If the old skin didn't come off, he would be locked into the same stage of life forever. The top skin must die in order for new growth to manifest itself.

The Lord has given us his Holy Spirit for the same reason. He will gently speak to your heart and let you know when it's time to grow. He will urge you to get rid of the old things that are keeping you from growth. Are you willing to listen to the voice of the Holy Spirit? If not, you will not experience the growth you need in your Christian walk.

Have you ever noticed how the praying mantis folds his hands close to his head almost as if he is praying? How often do your friends and family members see you in this posture? Spiritual growth comes with time spent with the Lord. It comes by us allowing the Holy Spirit to manifest to our hearts the things we need to put off.

If so be that ye have heard him, and have been taught by him, as the truth is in Jesus: That ye put off concerning the former conversation the old man, which is corrupt according to the deceitful lusts; And be renewed in the spirit of your mind; And that ye put on the new man, which after God is created in righteousness and true holiness. Wherefore putting away lying, speak every man truth with his neighbour: for we are members one of another. Be ye angry, and sin not: let not the sun go down upon your wrath: Neither give place to the devil. Let him that stole steal no more: but rather let him labour, working with his hands the thing which is good, that he may have to give to him that needeth. Let no corrupt communication proceed out of your mouth, but that which is good to the use of edifying, that it may minister grace unto the hearers. And grieve not the holy Spirit of God, whereby ye are sealed unto the day of redemption. Let all bitterness, and wrath, and anger, and clamour, and evil speaking, be put away from you, with all malice: And be ye kind one to another, tenderhearted, forgiving one another, even as God for Christ's sake hath forgiven you. (Ephesians 4:21-32)

BROKEN TRUST

Have you ever put your trust in someone that broke it? It's not an easy thing to build back trust, but it is possible.

What if someone has broken your trust repeatedly? This becomes even harder. Each time the person breaks your trust the wall between you becomes thicker.

Broken trust can be like a wound on your body. Each time you allow the person to come back and they are not trustworthy, it opens the wound deeper. The wound may have time to scab over and start to heal but when they hurt you once again, it breaks open and bleeds. Each time, if the wound hasn't had enough time to heal, the wound gets deeper and deeper.

If you allow a wound on your body to become festered and out of control, it can eventually lead to cancer. The same thing is true with a relationship that has been broken. There may be a period of time that you must walk away from that person or the relationship in order to keep the wound from getting out of control.

If you have ever been in a relationship like this, you know how deep the pain of broken trust can be.

Allowing this area to become festered and bleed repeatedly will eventually cause it to become cancerous. This sore will get to the point there is nothing that can heal it, except for the Lord.

We don't need to put our trust in mankind. People will always let us down. In Romans it says, "There is none good, no not one." When we put all our trust into one person, we are looking for failure.

We would never want to shut ourselves completely off from everyone. We need to live our lives to the fullest. We need to pack a tote bag and have it available for when people break our trust. We need to be sure to have plenty of forgiveness packed in that tote bag. Bring along mercy, kindness and hope. We may need to pack some grace and prayer for when this person breaks our trust. We need to reach into our bag and pull out whichever one of these things that will help us through this hard time.

There have been many times I have had to pull hope out of my tote bag when I felt forgiveness had been used up. Other times I may have pulled out some grace, prayer or peace from the bag in order not to verbally destroy the other person or myself. A few times I even had to pull out some tough love and use it.

Jesus Christ is the only one we should put our trust in. He is the only one that is perfect and the only one that will not let us down.

Trust ye not in a friend, put ye not confidence in a guide: keep the doors of thy mouth from her that lieth in thy bosom. For the son dishonoureth the father, the daughter riseth up against her mother, the daughter in law against her mother in law; a man's enemies are the men of his own house. Therefore I will look unto the LORD; I will wait for the God of my salvation: my God will hear me.

(Micah 7:5-7)

PRESSURES IN LIFE

Are you having battles and pressures in your life? Are you feeling defeated? We all go through difficult times. We can react to those times in different ways. We can run away from our problems or we can stand up and face them.

When we decide to stand up and face our problems, it can change our lives. Standing up and facing the difficult things in life can be tough. There is a wrong way to handle bad situations, so we need to be sure and spend time in prayer before trying to stand against our problems. If we are not careful, we will make things worse instead of better.

As I was thinking about problems and pressures in life I was reminded that at an early age I learned about how a pearl was created. I believe the Lord has given us examples in nature for us to ponder and learn from. These things do not just happen for any reason. The Lord desires that we study his word and his creation. He desires for us to live a happier, healthier life.

The pearl is a beautiful creation. A pearl is created inside of a shell in the depths of the ocean. The shell has many parasites and other things that try to attack it. The sand itself enters into the shell and acts almost like sand paper. This process is what causes the magnificent pearl to form. If the shell clamped shut and never experienced any of these irritants, a pearl would never form.

What actually takes place during the process of forming the pearl is amazing. An irritant enters into the mollusk and settles. The mollusk becomes irritated, starts to produce a sac of external mantle tissue cells, and it secretes calcium carbonate and conchiolin to cover the irritant. If this mollusk produced anything except for the calcium carbonate and conchiolin, a pearl would not be formed.

We need to find out exactly what we need to do in order to bring forth something beautiful in our lives. Needless to say, Satan would rather you choose what he has to offer – bitterness or revenge – in place of what the Lord has offered. The Lord has made available to us the very thing we are in need of.

If any of you lack wisdom, let him ask of God, that giveth to all men liberally, and upbraideth not; and it shall be given him. (James 1:5)

The scriptures say that wisdom is more valuable than rubies. There is only one way to get wisdom and that is to ask of God. We are going to need the wisdom of the Lord to help us handle these trials in our life and come out a beautiful creation.

Order my steps in thy word: and let not any iniquity have dominion over me. Deliver me from the oppression of man: so will I keep thy precepts. Make thy face to shine upon thy servant; and teach me thy statutes. Rivers of waters run down mine eyes, because they keep not thy law. Righteous art thou, O LORD, and upright are thy judgments. Thy testimonies that thou hast commanded are righteous and very faithful. My zeal hath consumed me, because mine enemies have forgotten thy words. Thy word is very pure: therefore thy servant loveth it. I am small and despised: yet do not I forget thy precepts. Thy righteousness is an everlasting righteousness, and thy law is the truth. Trouble and anguish have taken hold on me: yet thy commandments are my delights. The righteousness of thy testimonies is everlasting: give me understanding, and I shall live. (Proverbs 119: 133-144)

YOU WILL ONLY GO AS DEEP AS YOUR ROOTS

Have you ever noticed the differences in trees? Closing my eyes and remembering when we lived in Tennessee and Alabama when I was a child, I could almost see the trees. These trees grew larger there. They engulfed the highways and covered the landscaping. Their beauty was breathtaking.

When I was ten years old, my father paid me to memorize Psalm chapter one. This chapter comes to mind often because it has many riches stored within it. In verse three of this Psalm it says,

And he shall be like a tree planted by the rivers of water, that bringeth forth his fruit in his season; his leaf also shall not wither; and whatsoever he doeth shall prosper. (Psalm 1:3)

The root system is what makes a tree great. If a tree has a shallow root system when the storms come, the tree may be uprooted. Trees with shallow root systems have to be watered more often, and they have a hard time surviving during a drought. These things cause the tree to be more susceptible to disease.

The Lord tells us where we need to be planted – beside the rivers of water. We should get as close to Jesus as possible. After all, he is the Living Water. There are many ways we can do this. We can receive watering for our spirit and soul by attending church, bible studies or studying the word of God for ourselves. Our souls are also watered by listening to praise and worship music or other music that gives us the word of God.

As ye have therefore received Christ Jesus the Lord, so walk ye in him: Rooted and built up in him, and established

in the faith, as ye have been taught, abounding therein with thanksgiving. (Colossians 2:6-7)

If you desire to be deeply rooted in the Lord you will never do so unless you spend time with him. What is keeping you from doing this? We all want to gain strength but many of us are not willing to go through what it takes to achieve that. Getting our body under submission is not an easy thing to do.

The Lord gives us a tip in the verse shown above. He says, "Walk ye." He didn't say jump into it or run. Take it easy, just walk and enjoy the time you spend with him. Before you know it, you will find you love having walks with the Lord.

You will only go as deep as your roots, so don't let the things of the world keep you from being rooted and grounded in the Lord.

That he would grant you, according to the riches of his glory, to be strengthened with might by his Spirit in the inner man; That Christ may dwell in your hearts by faith; that ye, being rooted and grounded in love, May be able to comprehend with all saints what is the breadth, and length, and depth, and height; And to know the love of Christ, which passeth knowledge, that ye might be filled with all the fulness of God. Now unto him that is able to do exceeding abundantly above all that we ask or think, according to the power that worketh in us, Unto him be glory in the church by Christ Jesus throughout all ages, world without end. Amen. (Ephesians 3:16-21)

MISSIONS

On KLOVE radio this morning, they were talking all about missions and I began to pray for our son Josh. Josh is a staff pastor in Garland, Texas. The staff at his church had been searching out what missions are really about. The Lord led me to look even deeper at what my definition of missions was. This is what the Lord showed me:

MISSIONS

M - Myself
I - Invoking
S - Self
S - Sacrifice
I - In
O - Others
N - Needing
S - Salvation

Invoking is calling on God and unless we take the time to call on God for this, we will not truly be able to do missions sacrificially. I'm afraid that sometimes I give, but not sacrificially.

We are so blessed to have been given the gospel, nice homes, cars and wonderful vacations. Much of the time we forget there are millions of people dying daily and in need of a Savior. They are in need of someone to lift them out of the mire they are in and to help them find a loving relationship with the Lord Jesus Christ. That person they might need could be you.

Greater love hath no man than this, that a man lay down his life for his friends. (John 15:13)

119

LIFTING UP THE HANDS THAT FALL DOWN

And it came to pass, when Moses held up his hand, that Israel prevailed: and when he let down his hand, Amalek prevailed. But Moses' hands were heavy; and they took a stone, and put it under him, and he sat thereon; and Aaron and Hur stayed up his hands, the one on the one side, and the other on the other side; and his hands were steady until the going down of the sun. And Joshua discomfited Amalek and his people with the edge of the sword. (Exodus 17:11-13)

You, nor anyone you know of, may be fighting the kind of battle Moses fought in the book of Exodus. I am positive though, that you know people in your church, town or area that do have battles they are fighting.

Others may not be fighting battles but just need to know you are there for them.

There were many times over the past year that I turned to my friends and family members to help hold my hands up, symbolically speaking. As I was writing the blog and compiling my book each day, I was in constant need of prayer.

My faithful friends in North Carolina, South Carolina, Wisconsin, Michigan, Arkansas, Tennessee and Texas lifted me up continually. Without their constant support and prayers it would have been difficult for me to carry on.

None of us are exempt. We all need others who will lift us up and help us in our daily walk with the Lord. If you don't have someone in your life that lifts your hands up when they fall down, pray and ask the Lord to place someone into your life to fill this void.

HOW'S YOUR WIRING?

There are times in our lives we need to stop and ask ourselves this question, "How is my wiring?" The Lord created us in his image, he created us to love, praise and serve him. He created us for his glory.

On the sixth day the Lord created mankind. He breathed into him the breath of life. When he gazed upon his creation he said, "This is very good." When God was finished, he looked at the completed project and realized all the wires had been connected correctly and everything was set to run smoothly.

It didn't take Adam and Eve long to make a mess out of things. It would be nice if it was only Adam and Eve that decided to rewire things. Are we not the same as Adam and Eve? We always want our own way. We have desires that feed our own flesh instead of praising the one who created us.

Where did we go wrong?

Where did we get our wires crossed?

This process begins slowly and, before we know it, we have strayed so far from the Lord that other people wouldn't even recognize our original creator.

If you were an engineer and produced a radio, would you want to find out later on that the wires got switched down the assembly line? The radio ended up making noises like a blow dryer instead of playing music due to the change.

What about you as a parent, would you be shocked to hear your infant barked instead of cried?

We would be taking the child to the doctor's office immediately to find out what is wrong with it.

Should we not be as concerned about ourselves?

LET EVERYTHING THAT HATH BREATH PRAISE THE LORD

God created us to praise him and give him glory, yet we spend more time praising ourselves and making ourselves look good. We can't seem to find time to do the very thing we were created to do.

If you find this to be true in your own life, then it's time to go back to the manufacturer, the word of God, and see if he can't help you with your wiring. God's word says we are fearfully and wonderfully made. Let's not get our wires crossed.

I will praise thee; for I am fearfully and wonderfully made: marvellous are thy works; and that my soul knoweth right well. (Psalm 139:14)

WHAT DOES YOUR PRAISE LOOK LIKE?

Where do you find happiness? Is it in your car, house, or job? There is more depression in the 21th Century than ever before. What has happened to our joy?

When the Pilgrims came over on the Mayflower they had nothing. They had no homes to live in, no beds to sleep in and no cars to drive. Yet we see that they set aside a celebration time in order to give thanks to God for helping them settle in this great land.

They looked to God for their provisions and he provided.

In the 21st Century, families often have two or three cars. Some have huge houses but also own cabins or summer homes, all of which are decked with expensive items. Yet we seem much more ungrateful than the generations before us who had virtually nothing.

We continue to hoard and gather increase so we can look better than others. We should, in fact, be doing as the Native Americans, taking the time to help others out, even if we don't know them. Do others have to be like us before we help them? No, they don't have to be of the same skin color or from the same denomination. We need to have a heart for people in need.

David continually praised God for all he had been given. He took the alphabet and told of the goodness of the Lord in Psalm 119. It might do us good to do as David and write down our thanksgivings based on the twenty-six letters of our alphabet.

LET EVERYTHING THAT HATH BREATH PRAISE THE LORD

We are blessed far more than any nation or previous generation, therefore we should be able to praise so much better. What does your praise look like?

Be still, and know

that I am God:

I will be exalted

among the heathen,

I will be exalted in the earth.

(Psalms 46:10)

CHANGING YOUR VIEW

Life is filled with so many trials, defeats and problems. Each of these trials will shape our lives. While reading about photography, I saw an obvious lesson we could learn.

This lesson helps us see exactly who God is. We can plainly see that it's not about getting the Lord Jesus Christ to change when we go through the trials of life but how we view those trials.

When taking a picture, in order to capture the perfect reflection in water, there are certain things a photographer has to take into consideration.

> ➤ The least little ripple in the water will cause the picture to be distorted. The stillness of the water is the key to taking a better picture.
> ➤ A steady hand is necessary. The slightest shake or wobble will cause the picture to be distorted.

Thus we see why the scripture says:

> *Be* still*, and know that I am God: I will be exalted among the heathen, I will be exalted in the earth. (Psalms 46:10)*

We need to listen closely to this verse, because we will not be able to get a true sight of the Lord unless we quit causing ripples in the water. Stress in our lives can cause us to be unsteady and give us a distorted view. When we see his reflection in the water, we aren't really sure it's the Lord.

> ➤ The position the photographer gets into is vital when taking photographs. To get the best image you will need to kneel down or lay down.

This truth helps us to understand some of the scriptures better:

O come, let us worship and bow down: let us kneel before the LORD our maker. (Psalm 95:6)

And thus are the secrets of his heart made manifest; and so falling down on his face he will worship God, and report that God is in you of a truth. (I Corinthians 14:25)

➤ If other lights are used in trying to get a perfect picture, many times light will just bounce off the water. Therefore, when the photo is developed, one will not be able to see the reflection.

There are so many times when we are going through trials that we search in every direction instead of looking into the word of God, the true light. Then we wonder where the Lord is. Yet, all the time it was our own fault we couldn't see the presence of God.

➤ Preventing double images can be obtained by standing in a certain direction. The photographer can actually capture a double view of the reflection if he positions himself incorrectly.

How many times do you remember hearing somebody explain how horrible their situation was? When you look at the same situation, it looks so minor. Then there are times a person has been through a very traumatic experience yet they seem to think it was nothing. It all depends on where we are standing and how we allow the Lord Jesus Christ be reflected in our lives.

Jesus saith unto him, Have I been so long time with you, and yet hast thou not known me, Philip? He that hath seen me hath seen the Father; and how sayest thou then, Shew us the Father? (John 14: 9)

The Lord is asking, "Why haven't you seen the reflection?"

After all, he did set the stage for a perfect picture. God, being above and the Lord Jesus Christ, being the Living Water,

Philip should have been able to plainly see the reflection. Philip had probably looked in so many directions trying to figure it out, but failed to get on his knees.

Are we not just like Philip?

Let's not miss this next point. We were created to be a reflection of Jesus Christ.

When others see our lives, do they see the same image of Christ? If not, we need to ask the Lord to help us better reflect who he is to our world

So God created man in his own image, in the image of God created he him; male and female created he them.

(Genesis 1:27)

WHAT WILL YOU
MAGNIFY TODAY?

Each day, as we wake, we are faced with the same question. Unaware we are faced with it, we go about getting dressed as usual. We start with a shower, putting on a cup of coffee and grabbing a bite to eat. Little do we know we are going to magnify something today. It is just going to happen. You don't have to plan it out.

Someone calls on the phone and begins to tell us something that happened yesterday. As we hear this piece of news we naturally start to dissect the information.

Where did it happen?

Why did they do that?

What is it going to profit?

And then, who all was involved?

Each piece of information that goes through our mind gets put under a microscope. We have the need to dissect the data in order to understand it properly. After understanding it, we are faced with a discussion of, "What are we going to do with the information now?"

Many people will only dissect it themselves but there are others who will call someone else and magnify the information to them. In turn, the next person will do the same thing, properly dissecting it in their mind and passing along the knowledge. Each of us dissect data differently thus by the time the story comes back around to the actual person it was about, it isn't even recognizable.

Have you ever heard anyone make the statement, "She blows everything way out of proportion?" Meaning, she makes everything seem big. I'm sure we all have been guilty at one point or another of magnifying something more than it should be.

There are many wounded people out there that have been the victims to this sort of thing. We do it openly in conversations and act as if it's normal. We need to guard against this in our churches and Christian lives.

There are many times newcomers or new Christians come to me and are shocked this happens so openly during fellowship time, while we are cooking, cleaning, or setting things up for Vacation Bible School. Yet at the same time we as Christians are too afraid to magnify the Lord. What is the matter with us?

It amazes me when Christians scolds another for praising God in a certain way and then a week later you hear the same person with profanity or gossip coming out of their mouth.

Let us scold the profanity and gossip and encourage worship and praise.

Did you know most people that get wealthy were big thinkers? These are people who could see in their minds things bigger and better.

If we minimize ourselves, we tend to meet up to how we feel about ourselves. On the other hand if we magnify ourselves, we have a tendency to stretch and try to achieve the goal we have magnified ourselves to. Although we see there is a limit to even this.

For I say, through the grace given unto me, to every man that is among you, not to think of himself more highly than he ought to think; but to think soberly, according as God has dealt to every man the measure of faith. (Romans 12:3)

We are not to magnify ourselves too high as we see those who think they are greater than God himself.

LET EVERYTHING THAT HATH BREATH PRAISE THE LORD

Let them be ashamed and brought to confusion together that rejoice at mine hurt: let them be clothed with shame and dishonor that magnify themselves against me.

(Psalm 35:26)

And the LORD said, Behold, the people is one, and they have all one language; and this they begin to do: and now nothing will be restrained from them, which they have imagined to do. Go to, let us go down, and there confound their language, that they may not understand one another's speech. So the LORD scattered them abroad from thence upon the face of all the earth: and they left off to build the city. Therefore the name of it is called Babel...

(Genesis 11:6-9)

There are definitely times we should magnify certain things. Here are the things we should magnify. We should take the time to magnify the Lord as the psalmist said.

O magnify the LORD with me, and let us exalt his name together. (Psalm 34:3)

Magnify in this verse means to increase, glorify, lift up and show forth his magnificence, splendor, grandeur and sublimity.

The Lord isn't proud; he just knows who he is. The following verse shows us this truth.

"Thus will I magnify myself, and sanctify myself; and I will be known in the eyes of many nations, and they shall know that I am the LORD." (Ezekiel 38:23)

We all need to take time to see if we are magnifying the Lord above all as we see he truly is magnificent and worthy of our praise. If we are spending our time magnifying the Father, we will spend less time magnifying things that do not need to be magnified.

GETTING THE WORD OF GOD INTO PEOPLE'S HEART

Have you ever noticed that when people repeat bad things often, their words tend to get programmed into our minds?

When you hit your thumb and kick your toe on the bed, what words tend to come to mind? The reason for this is that we have been programmed by friends and family.

I once had a friend that said "piffle" each time something bad happened. To this very day, I catch myself saying "piffle." People look at me funny and ask what does "piffle" mean.

Piffle (noun) Nonsense, silly talk or ideas.

Piffle (intransitive verb) Behave thoughtlessly, To behave in a silly or ineffective way.

Give your friends and family something to think about – JESUS!

The same is true for them if you spend a lot of time saying godly things, quoting a scripture, or leading them to Christ. They may not all follow through and trust the Lord but one thing is for sure; your words will play back in their minds as much as theirs do in your mind.

Whom shall he teach knowledge? and whom shall he make to understand doctrine? them that are weaned from the milk, and drawn from the breasts. For precept must be upon precept, precept upon precept; line upon line, line upon line; here a little, and there a little: (Isaiah 28:9-10)

WHAT ARE YOU WRAPPED UP IN?

It's so easy to get wrapped up in the holidays and the hustle and bustle of shopping, cooking, wrapping presents and placing them under the tree. Our greatest need is for us, ourselves to be wrapped up.

We need to allow the Savior to wrap his arms of love around us. When people look at our lives during the holiday seasons, may we radiate with these beautiful wrappings.

➢ Diligence
➢ Kindness
➢ Godliness
➢ Patience
➢ Charity
➢ Faith
➢ Temperance
➢ Virtue

According as his divine power hath given unto us all things that pertain unto life and godliness, through the knowledge of him that hath called us to glory and virtue: Whereby are given unto us exceeding great and precious promises: that by these ye might be partakers of the divine nature, having escaped the corruption that is in the world through lust. And beside this, giving all diligence, add to your faith virtue; and to virtue knowledge; And to knowledge temperance; and to temperance patience; and to patience godliness; And to godliness brotherly kindness; and to brotherly kindness charity. (II Peter 1:3-7)

Whom have I in heaven but thee?
and there is none upon earth
that I desire beside thee.
My flesh and my heart faileth:
but God is the strength of my heart,
and my portion for ever.
(Psalm 73:25-26)

LET EVERYTHING THAT HATH BREATH PRAISE THE LORD

Made in the USA
Columbia, SC
28 August 2021